A WARTIME LOG

A REMEMBRANCE
FROM HOME
THROUGH THE AMERICAN Y.M.C.A.

Original design courtesy the World Alliance of Y.M.C.A.s

Besides ever present danger, the Army Air Force prisoners of war faced daily boredom. They combatted it with a variety of diversions, including playing cards. Robert McVicker's Wartime Log *contained this drawing of the time-consuming activity in a typical barracks room.*

THE NEW THEATER
SOUTH COMPOUND—STALAG LUFT III
PRESENTS

STRICTLY
FROM
HUNGER

A Musical Review in Three Acts

DIRECTED BY IRVING S. BIRNS

Musical Dir-

Music Arrang-
R.D. Dougla-

American P.O.W.s formed theater groups and staged productions. Programs (left) were printed when paper was available and productions such as Life With Father *(below) featured sets designed and produced by the prisoners. The seats (right) in* Stalag Luft I *were empty wooden Red Cross shipping crates.*

(THEATER PROGRAM COURTESY THOMAS C. GRIFFIN, THEATER PHOTOS COURTESY JACK FRIEND)

Lt. C. H. Holmstrom, a prisoner in Stalag Luft III, *was an accomplished artist who captured the essence of camp life in these two pencil drawings. Prisoners maintained a schedule of daily chores including washing clothes and airing blankets. In their spare time, which sometimes seemed endless, a book from the camp library helped to pass the hours.*

(COURTESY YMCA OF THE USA ARCHIVES,
UNIVERSITY OF MINNESOTA LIBRARIES)

Red Cross officials periodically visited the camps to ensure that Geneva Convention provisions were being honored by the Germans. This photo was taken in a Stalag Luft III barracks by Red Cross officials. The men were identified as, from left to right (top) Lieutenants D. J. Maher and J. A. Dorfman and (bottom) Lieutenants Linden Price, A. H. Wiench, R. C. Cecil, H. E. Kious and J. A. Bartlett.

A WARTIME LOG

BY ART AND LEE BELTRONE

HOWELL PRESS

ACKNOWLEDGMENTS

Several years ago my friend, Ed Archer, sent me a *Wartime Log* book to identify. In more than forty years of studying military history and collecting military artifacts, I had never seen such a remarkable journal. Its pages were covered with carefully placed poetry and collections of information, as well as pencil drawings and vibrant watercolors. That book started me on a three-year-long worldwide search for other log books. The results of that search served as the foundation of this book.

This work was made possible with the help of former prisoners of war and their family members who were willing to share their *Wartime Log* books or historical accounts. I am grateful for the cooperation provided by John H. Adams, Jr., Hardy Z. Bogue III, Joseph Boyle, Claire Cline, Joseph DiMare, Dorothy Fishburne, Jack Friend, Bettie Frye, Col. Francis Gabreski, Thomas C. Griffin, William H. Harvey, Henry Gorski, Robert Keller, Leonard H. Kessinger, Arthur G. Kroos, Jr., Elmer T. Lian, James Mankie, Robert McVicker, Alex Palmer, R. T. Peterson, Orvis Preston, Patrick P. Reams, Al Ricci, William Rolen, Leonard Rose, Angelo M. Spinelli, Richard Stewart, Michael Stroff, Roy E. Wendell, Charles M. Williams, Edward Wodicka, Daniel Wilkerson, and Hubert Zempke. Special thanks go to Robert A. Long of the Swiss Internees Association, James McMahon of the Association of Americans Interned in Sweden, Peter and Doris Murphy of the Virginia Chapter of American Ex-Prisoners of War, and Robert L. Weinberg of the *Stalag Luft* III Association. They provided invaluable assistance in locating former prisoners.

The following individuals and organizations also provided support: Margaret Adamic, the Walt Disney Company; Ed Archer, Jackie Berry, and Elizabeth Hooks of the American Red Cross Archives; John Burkhart, formerly of the Y.M.C.A., David Carmichael of the YMCA of the USA Archives; Claude-Alain Danthe of the World Alliance of Y.M.C.A.s; Sue Losinski at Brown & Bigelow; Charles Margosian; Arthur F. McGrandle; Elaine Miller at the Washington State Historical Society; Duane Reed of the Air Force

Academy Library; Henry Soderberg; Dr. Richard Summers, Chief Archivist-Historian at the U.S. Army Military History Institute; Fred Von Fricken; and Charles G. Worman of the Air Force Museum.

Collectors and historians shared information and items from their libraries and militaria collections. I thank F. Patt Anthony, Don Armstrong, Ron Burkey, Jr., Duncan Campbell, John Colgan, John Conway, Tony Fidd III, Norm Flayderman, John Gaertner, Al Gleim, Nancy Graham, Steve Griffith, Jack Hatter, Russell J. Huff, Phil Leveque, Ed Keller, Larry Martin, Thomas McVay, George Peterson, Russ Pritchard, Patrick Regis, Carl A. Robin, Alan Smith, Tony Stamatelos, Jeff Stevens, Jim Young, and Ray Zyla for their willingness to share and to assist when help was needed.

A number of people went well beyond simply helping. They were always there with information as well as logistical support, no matter what time of day or night. I am grateful to Neill Alford, Jr., Gary Alter, Tom Cutitta, Dr. Dieter H.M. Groschel, graphic designer Lotta Helleberg, Ross Howell of Howell Press, and editor Kate Neale. Dorothy Fishburne provided continuous and much appreciated assistance throughout the project, as did longtime friend Roy E. Wendell.

The help and support of my family also made this book possible. My wife, Lanenne (Lee) Beltrone, photographed the original *Wartime Log* book artwork. She worked tirelessly, patiently, and often in makeshift studio settings to document this remarkable representation of prison camp artwork. When not behind her camera she served as word processor, editor, counsel, critic, and, always, a friend. Continuous support was also provided by my children, Laurel and Brent Beltrone.

Finally, I wish to thank my late parents, Arthur and Marie Beltrone, for their encouragement of my interest in military history at an early age.

Art Beltrone
Keswick, Virginia
September, 1994

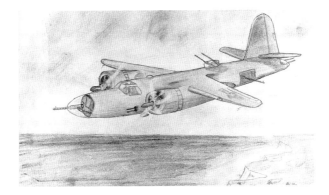

WORLD WAR II AMERICAN PRISONER OF WAR
& INTERNEE ASSOCIATIONS

Clydie Morgan
National Adjutant
National Headquarters
AMERICAN EX-PRISONERS OF WAR
3201 E. Pioneer Parkway, #40
Arlington, TX 76010-5396
(817) 649-2979

Bill Rolen
Executive Director
National Capitol Office
AMERICAN EX-PRISONERS OF WAR
1120 Vermont Avenue, NW
Washington, DC 20421
(202) 418-4258

Robert L. Weinberg
STALAG LUFT III ASSOCIATION
2229 Rock Creek Drive
Kerrville, TX 78028
(210) 257-4643

Leonard Rose
STALAG LUFT 4 ASSOCIATION
(also includes STALAG LUFT 6)
8103 E. 50th Street
Lawrence, IN 46226-2018
(317) 546-1860

Leonard H. Kessinger, Jr.
STALAG 17B ASSOCIATION
1106 Harrison Street
Princeton, WV 24740
(304) 425-7079

Robert A. Long
SWISS INTERNEES ASSOCIATION
69D Dorchester Drive
Lakewood, NJ 08701
(908) 901-0899

James McMahon
ASSOCIATION OF AMERICANS
INTERNED IN SWEDEN
PO Box 4954
Santa Rosa, CA 95402
(707) 578-4013

Designed by Lotta Q. Helleberg
Edited by Ross A. Howell, Jr. and Katherine A. Neale

Printed in China
Published by Howell Press, Inc., 1147 River Road, Suite 2, Charlottesville, Virginia 22901.
Telephone (804) 977-4006.
First Printing

Library of Congress Cataloging-in-Publication Data

Beltrone, Art, 1941-
    A Wartime log / Art and Lee Beltrone, p. cm.
    Includes bibliographical references and index.
    ISBN: 0-943231-90-6.

1. World war, 1939-1945—Personal narrative, American. 2. Prisoners of war—United States.
3. World war, 1939-1945—Prisoners and prisons, German. I. Beltrone, Lee, 1942- II. Title.

D811.A2B45 1995   940.54`8173
                                    QB194-21155

CONTENTS

Former American Air Force prisoners of war are all smiles following the liberation of Stalag Luft I, Barth, Germany *(opposite page).* Stalag Luft III *prisoners who were moved to Stalag 7A at Moosburg are shown after their liberation preparing food from a special Red Cross truck convoy. Pilot Robert Keller stirs the mixture while fellow officer Andrew Anderson operates the special prisoner-made machine called "Kriegie blower," which heated the food.*

(COURTESY DOROTHY FISHBURNE
AND ROBERT KELLER)

Introduction	14
Part I Off to War	23
Alone But Not Forgotten	27
The Birdmen	34
Help From Home	36
One Mission Too Many	37
Bailout Over Cologne	45
Part II For You the War Is Over	49
Name, Rank, and Serial Number	65
Caged Birdmen	70
The Geneva Convention	71
The Prisoner	77
Part III Camp Life	81
Food For Thought	97
Kriegie Recipes	102
Wanted: A Wartime Log	104
The Art of Living	108
Art Students	110
Escape of the Poet-Artist	117
Rumor Mill	119
Hurtful Humor	121
Passing Time	122
Let's Make a Deal	126
Part IV Confound and Confuse	129
The Show Must Go On	131
Behind the Scenes	132
War of Wits	146
Lead Wings and Tin Plates	152
The Sound of Music	156
Part V Can It Be Over...	161
Journey to Liberation	162
A Friendlier Spotlight	168
The Tour	170
Appendix	174
Bibliography	204
Index	206

INTRODUCTION

A *Wartime Log* was a most unusual book, written and illustrated by American prisoners of war. *Wartime Log* books are a collective memoir of life behind barbed wire during World War II.

While the cover of each book was the same, the contents differed because each one of the volumes represented an individual's likes and dislikes, his optimism and pessimism. Book entries, whether written or illustrated, were often made without adequate writing or drawing materials. Pencils were begged or bartered for and brushes were frequently made from human hair. Coloring for drawings was extracted from ersatz German coffee grounds or the colored labels from cans in Red Cross food parcels. In prison camps American ingenuity had to be utilized on an everyday basis.

The writers and artists were United States Army Air Force pilots and aircrew members who had been participants in the air war over Europe, the most extensive and deadly aerial combat of the twentieth century. More than thirty thousand airmen were forced to earth by enemy aircraft, ground fire, or mechanical malfunctions in their planes. Sitting behind the barbed wire fence enclosures of German prison camps, they were without many of life's necessities. The lack of food was paramount, so the Red Cross organized to provide life-sustaining nourishment in the form of food parcels.

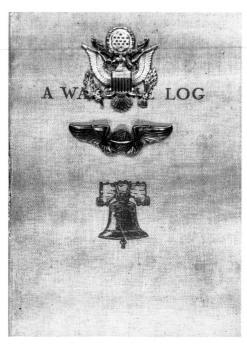

Paper and writing implements were in very short supply and the Young Men's Christian Association (Y.M.C.A.), through its War Prisoners Aid organization, developed programs to maintain the physical and mental health of each captive. One such program was the creation and distribution of the *Wartime Log* books.

The books were printed in Switzerland and delivered to the air and ground force camps by Y.M.C.A. and Red Cross officials. There, they were distributed to the prisoners who were encouraged to use the books to record personal thoughts, daily events, poetry, short stories, and artwork. Although *Wartime Log* books were distributed to P.O.W.s in all branches of the service, only books maintained by U.S. Army Air Force prisoners have been included in this study.

The airmen, many of whom were quite young, had defied death more than twenty thousand feet above the earth during terror-filled missions that took them to the very heart of Germany. They watched helplessly as less fortunate friends were blown from the sky by enemy fighters or ground fire. As the air war intensified, the number of Army Air Force prisoners grew significantly.

According to Geneva Convention provisions, as commissioned and noncommissioned officers, members of flight crews were not required to perform manual labor while held captive. Instead they

The title page of B-17 tail gunner Sylvan Cohen's *Wartime Log* features a drawing of the bomber on which he served.
(COURTESY HARDY Z. BOGUE III)

The second page of each *Wartime Log* (right) had several blank lines on which the P.O.W. was to record his name.
(COURTESY BELTRONE COLLECTION)

At far left navigator Edward Wodicka's *Wartime Log*. He attached his cap insignia and wings to the front cover.
(COURTESY EDWARD WODICKA)

A WARTIME LOG

A REMEMBRANCE
FROM HOME
THROUGH THE AMERICAN Y.M.C.A.

Published by
THE WAR PRISONERS' AID OF THE Y. M. C. A.
37 Quai Wilson
Geneva — Switzerland

THIS BOOK BELONGS TO

Y.M.C.A.

faced the drudgery of the camp's daily routine, month after frustrating month. Details about specific prisons can be found in the appendix, which contains official government reports about camps holding U.S. Army Air Force prisoners. Books written by former prisoners about specific camps can be found in the bibliography and a list of prisoner of war associations is included on page 11.

A Wartime Log provided a mental escape from physical imprisonment. Each man's comments and drawings represent his dream of freedom and his hope for the future. The books have been closely guarded over the years by former P.O.W.s or their loved ones who inherited the volumes, so the existence of such personal records has, until now, been virtually unknown.

Several years of research and thousands of miles of travel uncovered more than a dozen *Wartime Log* books, still in the hands of former prisoners of war. While each of the books located tells a separate, personal story, they all share a number of

common characteristics—the prisoner's patriotism, his sense of humor, his creativity, and his will to survive.

This *Wartime Log* is published to commemorate the fiftieth anniversary of the liberation of U.S. Army Air Force prisoners of war. It contains a selection of the writing and artwork placed in the original books by Americans imprisoned in German camps. (Little reference is made to the many escape tunnels dug by prisoners. Prisoners did not include such entries in their *Wartime Log* books because German camp officials regularly inspected the journals.) Archival photographs documenting the progression of the war are also included.

It is to all American prisoners of war, all those patriots who refused to surrender hope and were unswerving in their loyalty to country and fellow prisoners, that this commemorative *Wartime Log* is dedicated.

WAR PRISONERS AID

AIDE AUX PRISONNIERS DE GUERRE

KRIEGSGEFANGENENHILFE

WORLD'S ALLIANCE OF YOUNG MEN'S CHRISTIAN ASSOCIATIONS
ALLIANCE UNIVERSELLE DES UNIONS CHRÉTIENNES DE JEUNES GENS
WELTBUND DER CHRISTLICHEN VEREINE JUNGER MÄNNER

GENÈVE (Suisse)
Centre international
37, Quai Wilson

Adresse Télégraph.: FLEMGO-GENÈVE
Compte de Chèques postaux: I. 331

April, 1945

Dear Friend,

As its title-page indicates, this book comes to you through the War Prisoners' Aid of the Y.M.C.A., as part of its service to prisoners of war all over the world. This service consists of visitation to the camps by Y.M.C.A. representatives and the provision of books, educational materials, musical instruments, athletic and theatrical supplies and aids to worship. In our service to American prisoners the Special Service and Information Division has contributed a considerable amount of the material. The total work has been generously supported by the public through the National War Fund, so that this log-book is really a gift from the folks at home

If you do not want to keep a regular diary or even occasional notes on war-time experiences, these pages offer many other possibilities. If you are a writer, here is space for a short story. If you are an artist, you may want to cover these pages with sketches or caricatures from your camp. If you are a poet, major or minor, confide your lyrics to these pages. If you feel that circumstances cramp your style in correspondence you might write here letters unmailable now, but safely kept to be carried with you on your return. The written text might be a commentary on such photographs as you may have to mount on the special pages for that purpose. The mounting-corners are in an envelope in the pocket of the back cover Incidentally, this might be used for clippings you want to preserve, or, together with the small envelopes on the last page, to contain authentic souvenirs of life in camp.

Perhaps you will discover some quite different use for this book. Whatever you do, let it be a visible link between yourself and the folks at home, one more reminder that their thoughts are with you constantly If it does no more than bring you this assurance, the „Log" will have served its purpose.

Yours very sincerely,

WAR PRISONERS' AID OF THE Y.M.C.A.

Each *Wartime Log* was accompanied by a cover letter that suggested how it might be used by the prisoner.

(COURTESY WORLD ALLIANCE OF Y.M.C.A.S)

Patrick Reams affixed a variety of lead insignia made by prisoners at *Stalag Luft* I to the front and back covers of his *Wartime Log*. The front cover features a pilot's wing with "POW" within the shield and a small lead airplane in the upper right corner. The object below the Liberty Bell is a token commemorating Barth, Germany, the town nearest to the prison camp. The back cover of copilot Reams's book was titled "Wings of Freedom" by the aviator, who affixed a camp-designed P.O.W. wing with a parachute at the top (one wing is broken) and the wings of several Allied air forces at the bottom.

(COURTESY PATRICK REAMS)

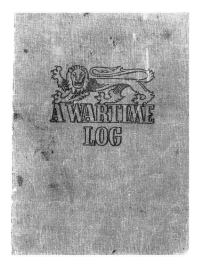

The "Y" also produced *Wartime Log* books for British and Canadian P.O.W.s. The British editions were smaller and had a lion on the cover; Canadian *Wartime Log* books had a maple leaf on the front.

(COURTESY DANIEL WILKERSON)

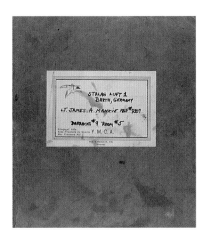

The Y.M.C.A. also provided prisoners with a small, soft-covered book with blank pages and a blue cover. Pilot James Mankie received one at *Stalag Luft* I—his entries included poetry and recipes.

(COURTESY JAMES MANKIE)

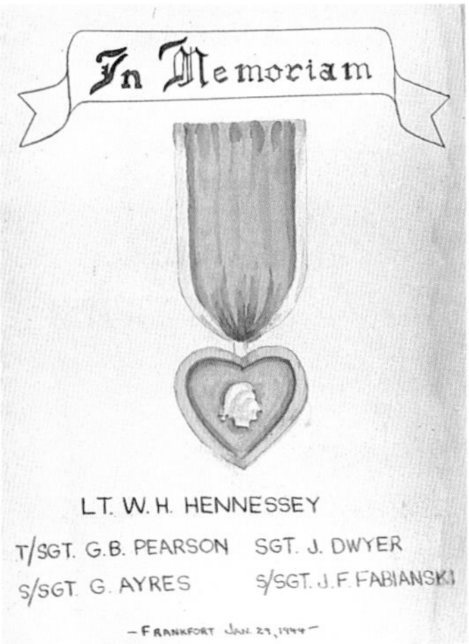

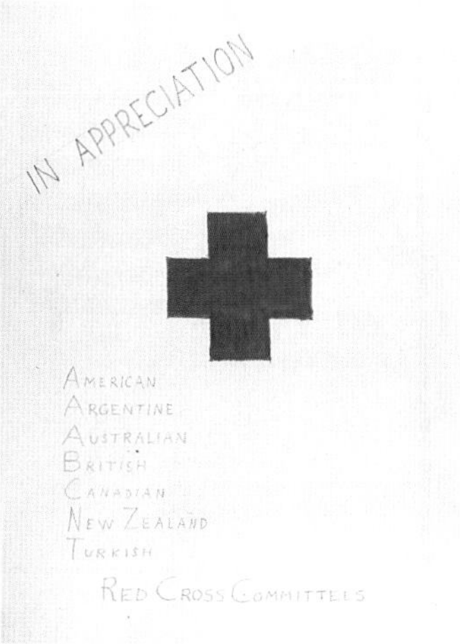

WITH GRATITUDE

Y.M.C.A.

In Memoriam

LT. W. H. HENNESSEY

T/SGT. G.B. PEARSON   SGT. J. DWYER

S/SGT. G. AYRES   S/SGT. J.F. FABIANSKI

— FRANKFORT Jan. 25, 1944 —

IN APPRECIATION

American
Argentine
Australian
British
Canadian
New Zealand
Turkish

Red Cross Committees

OUR SPIRITUAL GUIDES

Stalag Luft #4   Germany

Catholic

Protestant

J. Sterley Jackson
% 26 Clarence Ave.
Clapham Park.
London. S.W.4

G. Rex Morgan - C.F.

Inchyford, Sketty
Swansea. S. Wales

IF IN MORTALS THERE BE LOVE, THIS
                                            IS IT.
THAT THEY SHOULD LIVE AND FIGHT
                    OR DIE TOGETHER.
IN TRUTH, IT SHOULD BE SAID:
AIRMEN DO NOT DIE.

FOR IN THE HEARTS OF THOSE WHO
          WEAR THE SILVER WINGS,
UPON THEIR HUMBLE BREASTS,
AND INVADE THE CRYSTALLINE BLUE
WITH WINGS OF STEEL,
WE STILL FLY IN CLOSE FORMATION—
WITH THOSE WHO FLY ON ANGEL'S WINGS.

— LT. L.J. COLEMAN, R.C.W.

The first few pages of a *Wartime Log* often feature patriotic drawings and memorials to fallen comrades. Tail gunner Sylvan Cohen's book includes the patriotic drawing at left. Copilot Patrick Reams paid tribute to the Y.M.C.A., the Red Cross, and the American flag. Navigator Roy Wendell painted a Purple Heart medal with the names of deceased crew members. Flight engineer Richard H. Stewart listed his camp's ministers next to a drawing of a crucifix.

(COURTESY HARDY Z. BOGUE III, PATRICK REAMS, ROY E. WENDELL, RICHARD H. STEWART)

ENGLISH BROOK

Prisoner Richard Stewart included a painting of an English country scene (above) and a flowering plant (lower left) in his *Wartime Log*, while Edward Wodicka painted lilies in his book (above left). For many prisoners, artwork provided an escape from the reality of the prison camp. The German war flag, documented on one page of Claudius Belk's *Wartime Log* (right), was ever present.

~A Childs Soliloquy~

You won't be coming back I guess,
to see this pretty yellow dress.
    You know- I sorta thought you would
    'Cause I have been so very good.
Nobody ought to be away,
I think, on Jesus' Christmas day.
    I wonder why they have a war?
    What are little children for?
My poor dear mommie cries and cries,
But I'm a big girl for my size.
    And I remember what you said
    'Bout crying - So I won't, instead.
Gee, I hope you don't pain
I hope they keep you from the rain

of all the men on land and sea
They had to take the one from me
    If I could wish upon a star,
    I bet I'd fly to where you are.
But I'm so awful little gee-
No one pays any mind to me
    That's why I kinda miss you dad
    You was the bestes' friend I had
You was the goodes- looking man,
In all the world, from land to land,
    Mommie said that you would bring
    Me back a doll, and everything
But I know better than what they say
'Cause I know why you went away
    And I would rather have you back.
    And throw away my train and track.

My soldiers are upon the floor
I don't play soldiers any more
    Frank Stebbing, POW
        "OK"

~ "Stupidity and jealousy, the two black spots in human nature which more than love of
money, are the root of all Evil." "In the way it was not the fighting hero who were dominated
for peace, as has been said. "Hell hath no fury like a non-combatant." "Never ascribe to
an opponent motives meaner than your own." "Is as Walton quotes the saying that
the Almighty could have created a better than the Strawberry but that doubtless also he
Never did Doubtless also he could have provided us with better fun than hard work, but
I don't know what it is." "Unless a Man has Courage he has no security for preserving
any other Virtue." — from Courage - J.M. Barrie (1266

~ Raise the Crosses ~

Raise the Crosses, mark the grave heads
of all Nations fallen dead!
    Though we may not, God will tell them
    If or not they died in vain
And if earthly end misguided
Them to floods of fruitless pain
Raise the crosses without weeping
Safe's the host in heavens keeping!
    Let the living be more pitied
    For they live to cruelly kill
The inborn love of Man for brother
So they do, and so they will.
        Joseph B. Boyle.

Leaving the English coast, B-17 bombers head for a target somewhere in Germany. The aircraft, painted in Sylvan Cohen's *Wartime Log*, would soon be greeted by deadly flak and enemy fighters.

OFF TO WAR

A B-17, fire and smoke streaming from one engine, is captured in this drawing from Sylvan Cohen's log book. A German fighter circles above and watches the American craft's descent.

Battle Over Big B, painted by pilot C. Ross Greening while a prisoner in *Stalag Luft* I, epitomizes World War II aerial "hand-to-hand" combat. The scene, depicting more than 350 aircraft, took place over Berlin in 1944. Colonel Greening was an accomplished artist and shared his knowledge of drawing and painting with fellow prisoners. At war's end he received special recognition for his efforts from the Y.M.C.A.

(COURTESY DOROTHY FISHBURNE
AND BROWN & BIGELOW)

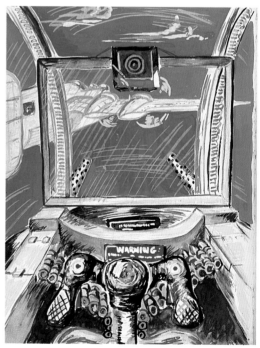

B-24 bombardier Jack Friend used watercolors and a brush made from his hair to show the view from his position in the aircraft's nose. Another B-24, en route to the same target, is visible from the bombardier's position.

(COURTESY JACK FRIEND)

CA poot !!

Views of German aircraft being destroyed and their airmen being wounded or killed were seldom placed on the pages of the *Wartime Log* out of fear of German authority. Tail gunner Sylvan Cohen, however, agreed to have this view of a Focke-Wulf pilot attempting to bail out of his burning aircraft placed in his book.

(COURTESY HARDY Z. BOGUE III)

The nose of the B-17 was equipped with .50-caliber machine guns that could be operated by the bombardier when under attack. The navigator served as an alternate gunner.

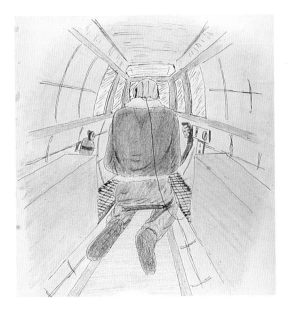

B-17 *Esquire's* tail compartment showing trays of .50-caliber ammunition and the cramped position of the gunner, who had to remain in this position for hours on end. Staff Sergeant Sylvan Cohen flew five missions at this dangerous post and was shot down on the sixth.

(COURTESY HARDY Z. BOGUE III)

The radio operator could use a single .50-caliber machine gun when under attack.

(COURTESY HARDY Z. BOGUE III)

ALONE BUT NOT FORGOTTEN

Sergeant Sylvan "Mike" Cohen, a street-wise twenty-five-year-old New Yorker, found himself in the cramped confines of a B-17G's tail gunner's compartment with his legs stretched under two .50-caliber machine guns. His post, away from the other crew members, was a lonesome place.

It was one of the most important defense points on the B-17G *Esquire*. The rear of the plane was a natural target for an enemy interceptor. Consequently, it was a dangerous spot for a crewman.

Sergeant Cohen, who changed his last name to Craig after the war, died in 1972, but his stepson, Hardy Z. Bogue III, thoughtfully recorded his military history after interviewing his stepfather and studying his *Wartime Log*. Cohen was a P.O.W. in *Stalag* 17.

Cohen had never flown before the war and after his sixth and final mission, he swore he would never fly again. Bogue explained that his stepfather, like all airmen, quickly learned about the dangers of his assignment. Aircraft loaded with fuel and explosives sometimes crashed and exploded during takeoff; others suffered a similar fate in flight after being hit by flak or projectiles from enemy planes.

"There was no real protection," Bogue recalls his stepfather saying of the aircraft's thin skin. "And the flak on occasion was very heavy. There

(Continued)

were often casualties and sometimes whole crews would die in a split second."

It is said there is comfort in numbers, but Sergeant Cohen sat all alone, watching the sky directly behind the *Esquire*, more than twenty thousand feet above the earth. The gunner knew that an enemy pilot would most likely attempt to eliminate him early in the aerial combat.

"He told me that in his position, he was cut off from the crew and that was what was so mind-boggling and so frightening," the stepson recounts.

"The other guys could see one another," Bogue says. "They were in contact with one another. But Mike was back in the tail of the aircraft by himself. He had to take his parachute off to get into that compartment. He could not fight with his parachute on. He would wait back there sometimes hours at a time for any kind of activity to take place. He was always very lonely back there. It was rough duty."

On 30 November 1943, during a mission over Solingen, Germany, the duty became extremely rough and the *Esquire* was shot down. Two crew members perished, but Mike Cohen survived and swore he would never fly again.

The accompanying color pictures were drawn in Cohen's *Wartime Log* by another prisoner. The tail gunner traded cigarettes and chocolate D-bars for the artwork.

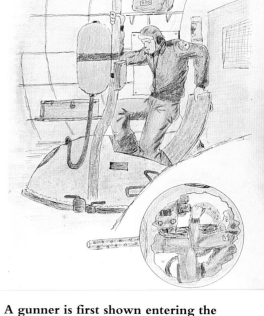

A gunner is first shown entering the *Esquire's* ball turret and in the firing position. The compartment, which could be entered from within the aircraft, was a Sperry ball power turret equipped with twin .50-caliber machine guns. It was located in the bottom of the B-17's waist section, just aft of the radio compartment. Men assigned to this position were usually smaller in size. They controlled the movement of the guns using hand and foot pedals.

(COURTESY HARDY Z. BOGUE III)

The pilot and copilot of the B-17 are shown flying to the target. The pilot flew the aircraft and commanded the plane and crew. The copilot, as described in the official B-17 pilot training manual, was the executive officer, the pilot's "chief assistant, understudy and strong right arm."

(COURTESY HARDY Z. BOGUE III)

One page in Sylvan Cohen's *Wartime Log* told the complete story of how an aviator became a prisoner. This watercolor shows a formation of bombers at the top and the enemy target burning below. Black puffs of flak greet the aircraft in a deadly game of "tag." A disabled B-17 heads for earth as the airman pulls the ripcord of his parachute. Another crew member has safely left the aircraft and opened his parachute and a yellow-nosed German Focke-Wulf Fw 190 passes overhead.

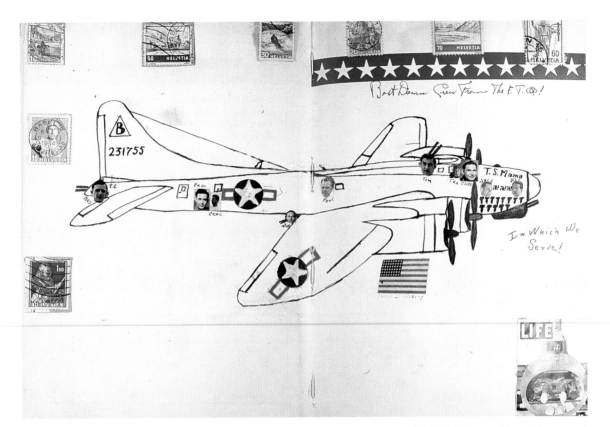

Best Damn Crew From The E.T.O.!

T.S. Mama

In Which We Serve!

(COURTESY BELTRONE COLLECTION)

Not all Americans who were shot down fell into the hands of the enemy—some landed in neutral countries where they became internees.

Wartime Log books were distributed to some of these men in Switzerland, Sweden, and other neutral countries. *Dottie G* ball turret gunner Joseph W.E. Martin received one while an internee in Switzerland. He drew a two-page spread of his aircraft in the book and added small photos of his fellow crew members to the pages.

According to Robert A. Long, president of the Swiss Internees Association, Sergeant Martin was shot down on 25 February 1944 after the *Dottie*

G was attacked by German Messerschmitt Bf 110 aircraft in the vicinity of Augsburg, Germany. After the B-17 dropped its bombs, smoke began to pour from two of its four engines. The pilot dove five thousand feet to successfully extinguish the flames. The airplane was brought under control, but when it reached the Swiss border it was hit by light flak from Swiss guns. Unable to continue, the aircraft landed at Dubendorf Air Field, near Zurich, and the crew members became Swiss internees.

There were 1,543 American internees in Switzerland and 1,218 in Sweden.

While a German fighter pilot smiles from above and asks "What's the matter, comrade?", an unhappy American in the form of a duck which resembles Disney's Donald Duck character floats in the sea and a burning aircraft plummets toward the water.

(COURTESY EDWARD WODICKA
USED BY PERMISSION OF THE WALT DISNEY COMPANY)

As the air war over Europe intensified, the Germans created a harrowing cartoon figure of an American aviator to evoke sympathy for their cause. The caricature had a large ring in his nose. Bombardier Jack Friend reproduced the figure in his *Wartime Log* with the following explanation, provided by the Germans: "A new air medal has been instituted by the USA in keeping with the cultural tradition of the land. It is worn in the nose."

(COURTESY JACK FRIEND)

"I got my Diploma right here- July 17, 1943."

The *Wartime Log* kept by Col. Ross Greening features a number of stunning watercolors, including this powerful account of his B-26 Marauder being shot down on 17 July 1943. The colonel parachuted safely and landed on the side of Mount Vesuvius. He was immediately captured but escaped two months later and spent the next six months evading the enemy by living in caves. He was eventually recaptured and spent the remainder of the war in *Stalag Luft* I.

(COURTESY DOROTHY FISHBURNE)

The best view of Vesuvius is right over it in a parachute. I landed ⅓ the distance from the top- Sure thought my goose was cooked!

AND WHO SHALL JUDGE?

Dropping bombs from dizzy heights
Upon a hapless foe,
Leaves flying men all unconcerned
To havoc wrought below.

For flying men are fighting men
Whose battles rage up where
Cold sunlight glints on spitting guns,
And fighters streak the air.

War's passion, hate and sentiment
Dissolve in frosty space,
And men are one with aeroplanes,
Nerves welded in the chase.

With boundless sky the battlefield
And measureless the gain,
Red blood flows free, as on the ground,
But never shows the stain.

The target reached, the bombs away,
Makes easier the mind
Whose single thought is getting home,
Not carnage left behind.

But what about the silent host
Who cheated death on high,
Who also thought their war was fought
In confines of the sky.

I cannot speak for lifeless forms
Strung up by silken shrouds
Of parachutes that saved them from
Fate's play above the clouds.

What speechless terror filled their minds
As by a mob they died,
Could not be told to you or me
Through cord so tightly tied.

But mute, grotesque, they clearly tell
What there is of pity
For luckless airmen dropping with
Bombs into a city.

And who's to judge the justice done
By hands that willingly
Stop digging for their buried dead
To rig a gallows tree.

— FROM JOSEPH B. BOYLE'S *WARTIME LOG*
(COURTESY JOSEPH B. BOYLE)

THE BIRDMEN

At one time there dwelleth in the land of the Saxons a group of strange men who flitteth here and there in the sky and madeth like birds for such was their business, to bring succor and protection to their brethren who lumbreth about on more unwieldy wings, and they were called "birdmen."

And one morning as the sun first shineth on the hut wherein the sleeping birdmen lay, the C.O. entered therein and he sayeth, "arise for the time of briefing is at hand." And he hastily departeth, for he was wise in the ways of the birdmen. And with much cursing and mumbling they arose, and appeaseth their tender bellies on fish heads and rice, for alas such was the manner of their quartermaster who walketh about on paddled feet.

Wherefore the birdmen wendeth their way to the briefing hut wherein they beheld strange markings on the wall. Many and numerous were the red spots on the plan of the enemy stronghold, and their gaze falleth to the handwriting on the wall, for such it was. And they sayeth one unto the other, "No, this cannot be!" And there was weeping and gnashing of teeth. And the sound of murmuring suddenly ceaseth as the Great Gray Owl entereth the room. He spake unto them saying, "Yea verily, wing upon wing of our big Friends must go forth this day and assaileth the enemy, and let us not laggeth behind, for he who stayeth is lost." And there was one among them called S-2 who claimeth to know the way of the enemy, but he spake to them in riddles and they believeth him not. But they sayeth one to the other, "Wherefore doth he speak thus, for he knoweth not, the odds by which we all reapeth it in the end." And spake still another to them of the winds and clouds but he confuseth them, and they needeth him not.

As they leaveth the briefing room some entereth the little house in great haste and still others enter the house in greater haste. Thus they departeth to their winged steeds, wherein they tangled themselves with many hoods and straps after a confusing manner. And each was known unto the others by various colors and numbers that they may know their places, and in this manner each after the other breaketh the bonds of earth. And one among them runneth fast but lefteth not, for his R.P.M. runneth out. And the others wondered at his good fortune. And another runneth home for his temperature riseth but he waxeth cold.

And as they cometh to the appointed place their big friends are gone before them and the birdmen are troubled, for lo, their fuel runneth out. And as they draweth nigh unto the target they behold many and numerous flashes among them and they weaveth and swoopeth to escape the flak, for such it was called. And Red I calleth The Great Gray Owl saying, "Whither shall we turn, canst not thou lead us out?"

And he replieth, "Oh ye of little faith, why dost thou murmur against me?"

And at this time great multitudes of the enemy birdmen descended on the big friends and the Forts were clobbered. For such was the custom of those days. And they calleth forth to other birds to come forth and give them succor, and they all came forth, save one who came fifth, for he spoke of a Focke-Wulf on his tail, whereupon each of the birdmen turneth this way and that way, and were lost one unto the other, and great confusion reigneth.

And Red I calleth to Red II saying, "Wherefore art thou, o Red II?" And Red II answereth saying, "Lo and behold I spinneth out and am lost to thee." Then they said one unto another, "Hitteth the silk," and the white parasols fluttereth to the earth.

Thus they came unto Kriegie Land. And here endeth the reading of the lesson.

— From Wartime Log *of First Lieutenant John Howard Adams,* Stalag Luft I, Barth, Germany. *A B-24 navigator, he was shot down during a bombing mission over Oldenburg, Germany, on 13 November 1943.*
(COURTESY JOHN HOWARD ADAMS)

**This pencil sketch from Robert McVicker's
Wartime Log shows a dogfight between
American and German fighters.**

(COURTESY ROBERT MCVICKER)

HELP FROM HOME

The original *Wartime Log* book produced for American prisoners by the War Prisoners Aid of the Y.M.C.A. contained 151 blank, numbered pages with 20 unnumbered sheets of heavier, darker paper as the book's center section. The book measured 7 1/4 inches wide by 9 1/2 inches tall and its cover was bound with a gray sailcloth. Imprinted on the front cover, over a rendering of the Liberty Bell, were the words *A Wartime Log* in maroon. A thin, blue silk bookmark was sewn to the top of the book's spine, and a stiff piece of paper, folded to form a rectangular pocket, was affixed to the inside of the back cover. Six cellophane envelopes, each 1 7/8 inches wide by 3 1/8 inches tall, were glued onto page 150. Twenty-one thousand books, each accompanied by a separate cover letter, were produced for American prisoners between 1943 and early 1945.

During the same time the Y.M.C.A. also produced 26,500 blank *Wartime Log* books for British and Canadian prisoners. The Canadian log was about the same size as the American log, but the British book was much smaller. The "Y" also sent a small, blank booklet with a soft, blue cover into the camps. It resembled

Y.M.C.A. workers pack books for shipment to American P.O.W.s in Europe.
(COURTESY YMCA OF THE USA ARCHIVES, UNIVERSITY OF MINNESOTA LIBRARIES)

a schoolchild's writing tablet and had a Y.M.C.A. label for the recipient to write his name in on the front cover.

Using donated funds the American Y.M.C.A. sent a vast array of educational, recreational, and spiritual articles to American prisoners of war in Europe. More than 650 item categories were represented, including sports articles (1,754,254 items), musical articles (244,232), and books (1,280,146). In addition, large quantities of handicraft materials, theatrical supplies, sewing machines, typewriters, film projectors, films, games, and religious articles were sent into the camps for the use of those held captive.

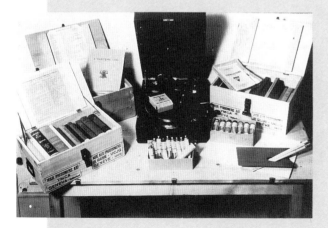

Y.M.C.A. supplies being readied for shipment to a German prison camp. A *Wartime Log* is visible in the box shown at upper left. In addition to books and art supplies, the Y.M.C.A. also provided phonographs.
(COURTESY YMCA OF THE USA ARCHIVES, UNIVERSITY OF MINNESOTA LIBRARIES)

ONE MISSION TOO MANY

The pre-mission wake-up call came at about four o'clock in the morning and got B-24 bombardier Chuck Williams, a member of the 762d Bomb Squadron, 460th Bomb Group, 15th Air Force, up from his bunk at the air base in Spinazolla, Italy. It was a routine he had been through thirty-five times before. Clean up, shave, eat breakfast, and attend the mission briefing. The thirty-sixth mission target—the rail yards at Vienna, Austria. The date—8 July 1944.

The crew of *Sweetie Girl* had completed thirty-five missions and could have gone home for R&R—rest and recuperation—before returning to combat, or they could forgo R&R, complete fifty missions and be done with their combat duty. The options were discussed and the crew decided to continue on.

With the briefing over and ten five-hundred-pound bombs aboard the aircraft, Williams and the rest of the crew tried to relax as the aircraft sped down the runway. Once airborne, *Sweetie Girl* and the other bomb group aircraft joined the main formation of approximately seven hundred bombers. As Williams's aircraft neared the IP, or Initial Point, the point at which the bombing run commences, he made the bombs ready for release. Subsequently he took control of the aircraft, standard procedure for bombardiers, who steered the plane until they reached the target and released the bombs. As *Sweetie Girl* approached the target, she was hit several times by flak. The damage was not serious.

"We released the bombs and they went into the target area," recalls Williams. A second or so after the bombs were away, the B-24 was badly

(Continued)

Navigator Edward Wodicka depicted his B-17's departure for combat in this humorous pencil drawing.
(COURTESY EDWARD WODICKA)

PRELUDE TO FLIGHT

In this pencil sketch, an aviator checks his aircraft before departing on a bombing mission. (COURTESY RICHARD H. STEWART)

hit by a burst of flak that knocked out the flight controls. The pilot struggled to hold the plane straight. It was a losing effort and *Sweetie Girl* started to lose altitude and fell out of the protected environment of the formation.

"We were alone," Williams recalls. "We were sitting out there."

They weren't alone for long. German fighter planes with yellow noses—Focke-Wulf Fw 190s and Messerschmitt Bf 109s—soon appeared, swooping down and firing on the disabled Liberator.

"At one point I counted eight of them doing a job on us," remembers the bombardier. "Our gunners shot down several of them." But the American bomber was going down. The copilot, the only crew member to carry a government-issued .45-caliber automatic pistol, blasted away at the fighters through his open window.

"It was just a gesture," Williams says of the action. "It probably made him feel better."

Williams, who had been on the flight deck standing behind the pilot and copilot, rushed to the plane's nose to retrieve his parachute. He did so without using a walk-around oxygen bottle. He had been off oxygen for some time when he kicked open the nose wheel door so he could leave the dying aircraft.

(Continued)

Germans attack a B-17 bomber in this pencil sketch from the *Wartime Log* of Richard H. Stewart, flight engineer on *The Baron*.

(COURTESY RICHARD H. STEWART)

Tail gunner Sylvan Cohen traded cigarettes or a chocolate D-bar for other prisoners' artwork. Ben Phelper drew Cohen in his cramped and lonely post in this cutaway pen and ink drawing.

(COURTESY HARDY Z. BOGUE III)

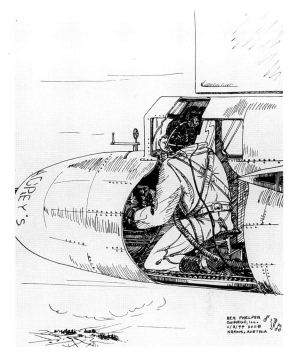

Ben Phelper drew Cohen's B-17 *Esquire* in pen and ink at *Stalag* 17B. The drawing covered two pages in Cohen's *Wartime Log*.

(COURTESY HARDY Z. BOGUE III)

The bombardier recalls kicking at the door and swinging in his parachute, safely away from the aircraft. But he remembers nothing in between.

"I probably passed out," he explains. "I was kicking to try to get the door open. The next thing I recalled I was swinging in my chute. I was free of the plane so I had obviously kicked the door open and as I kicked, fallen through the door. I obviously opened the parachute. I had to physically pull the ripcord on the chute. But I was swinging in the air."

Williams was terrified. He could no longer see *Sweetie Girl*, and he didn't see any other parachutes. But someone saw him.

"On the way down one of the [German] fighter pilots made three passes," Williams explains. "He would come in at me, and right before he would get to me he would rock up. As he would pass me, he would rock back. He was catching me in his prop wash and he was swinging me.

"He would swing me with the prop wash high enough that I was looking down at my parachute. Rather than shoot me he was trying to spill my chute. I would have dropped in clean. That way the records would have shown that the chute didn't open."

Fortunately, Williams was able to stabilize his parachute during the ordeal and he landed safely on the ground, where he was soon captured by a shotgun-wielding elderly civilian who used the weapon as a bat against the aviator's head, back, and side. The wounds—a broken ear drum, a compression fracture, and two broken ribs—weren't treated until Williams reached *Stalag Luft* I, his permanent prison camp.

DIE AMERIKANISCHER LUFT GÄNGSTER!

A B-17 with its right wing on fire over Avignon, France, begins its final plunge to earth. The surviving crew members found themselves before a German interrogator in a matter of days.

(COURTESY JEFF STEVENS)

U.S. bombers fly through black puffs of flak en route to a German target. The term "flak" comes from *Fliegerabweherkanone,* German for antiaircraft cannon.

(COURTESY BELTRONE COLLECTION)

An aerial combat cartoon from Edward Wodicka's *Wartime Log* shows that Germans viewed American aviators as "air gangsters." A damaged Allied bomber heads for earth in the background.

(COURTESY EDWARD WODICKA)

ADOLF HITLER ERKLÄRTE KRIEG

AN DIE VEREINIGTEN STAATEN

AM 11. DEZEMBER 1941

Die amerikanische Flugwaffe gibt die Antwort:

ANGRIFF

...Zusammen mit der RAF bei Tag und bei Nacht

...Auf kriegswichtige Ziele in allen Teilen des Reiches

DIESES FLUGBLATT WURDE VON EINEM AMERIKANISCHEN BOMBER ABGEWORFEN

USG 9

This propaganda leaflet was dropped from aircraft over Germany. The leaflet was titled "Day and Night With Combined Power" and read: "Adolph Hitler declared war on the United States on 11 December 1941—The American Air Force gives the response: ATTACK . . . together with the RAF by day and by night . . . on targets important for the war effort in all parts of the Reich. This leaflet was dropped by an American bomber." If civilians recovered the leaflets, they were to turn them over to local police or other government officials. Severe penalties, including death, could be levied on anyone caught passing leaflets to other civilians.

(COURTESY BELTRONE COLLECTION)

The last cartoon in navigator Edward Wodicka's series of *Wartime Log* pencil drawings emphasizes the uncertainty of the downed airman's future.

BRUNSWICK
100 KIL.

BAILOUT OVER COLOGNE

The German doctor, wearing a major's uniform, sat on the bed and broke the news to the twenty-three-year-old American Army Air Force flight engineer. The procedure to set the aviator's shattered ankle would have to be postponed. The major's brother had been killed during an air raid on Frankfurt and the officer was leaving to attend the funeral.

Sergeant Richard H. Stewart had been taken to the Catholic hospital, St. Elizabeth's Lazarette, just days before. The B-17 flight engineer's aircraft, *The Baron*, was returning from its mission against Bamberg, Germany, when it was hit by flak at twenty-eight thousand feet. It was 22 February 1944, the sixth mission for Stewart.

The plane had been hit late in the afternoon. With all four engines out of action, there was little choice but to leave the crippled ship. Stewart, slightly wounded from the flak, jumped through the open bomb bay door into the already darkening sky. He pulled the ripcord at an altitude of twenty-four thousand or twenty-five thousand feet.

"You couldn't see the ground at all," he remembers. "I had no idea where I was." The clouds were solid at the bailout altitude so there was no point in trying to steer his descent, he explains. And, because of the thin air at that altitude, the airman passed out for a short time due to lack of oxygen. He thought he could see land from about ten thousand feet, and as he got closer to the ground he found that snow was falling.

During his descent he noticed he was no longer wearing any boots. Just hours prior to the early-morning mission, the aviator had been in an English village near his air base, enjoying the pubs and other attractions. He had hurriedly returned to the airfield in order to attend the mission briefing, but was not in time to put on his usual flying gear. Stewart jumped into a heated flight suit without taking off his dress uniform and put a pair of insulated leather flying boots over his low-quarter shoes. The boots and shoes were stripped from his feet as he plummeted through the air before opening his parachute.

In bare feet he landed on the rubble-strewn pavement of a street—smack in the middle of Cologne, Germany—which had been subjected

(Continued)

B-17 flight engineer Richard H. Stewart added a self-portrait to his log book. His captors made these photos for his official identity card.

to the first one-thousand-bomber attack of the war on the night of 30-31 May 1942.

Stewart looked at his right foot and noticed it wasn't pointing forward. It now pointed to the rear, the result of a badly broken ankle. There was nowhere to hide, and there certainly was no way to run.

Civilians began to gather around the downed airman. They asked for his pistol, but he had none. A vehicle appeared and stopped near Stewart. It was occupied by two Luftwaffe officers and a woman.

"They picked me up and I sat up front with the driver," Stewart recalls. The other officer and the woman remained in the back seat. "The one in the back," the flight engineer explains, "he wasn't interested in me, he was interested in her."

Stewart was taken to St. Elizabeth's Lazarette and his ankle was temporarily immobilized until the doctor could return from his brother's funeral in Frankfurt.

The doctor, who had attended an American medical school, soon returned and Stewart was moved to the hospital's operating room and given an injection to induce sleep. He awoke to find his ankle bone reset. Weights surrounded his leg, keeping it stabilized. He remembers speaking to the doctor before the procedure, but the German had said nothing about the funeral.

"And I sure wasn't going to mention it," says the flight engineer.

The excitement surrounding the demise of *The Baron* and parachuting from the doomed aircraft clouded Stewart's mind.

"It was about three days before I realized exactly where I was and what was going on," he recalls.

The hospital was nearly full at the time. Many of the patients were civilians who had been badly burned during air raids. Because he wore striped pajamas, just like the rest of the patients, very few of them realized he was an American airman.

The nurses were nuns who treated the aviator kindly. A young woman who Williams believes was a hospital administrator brought him jugs of tea and containers of fruit.

"She'd go to Berlin every so often and come back and tell me about the train ride," Stewart recalls. The aviator was also warned about some staff members and officials who were sympathetic to the Nazi cause. "I was told who to be dumb to and who not to talk to."

Allied air raids occurred just about every day. Stewart's bed was in the hospital's basement, which also served as the air raid shelter. Whenever aircraft flew over the hospital, the basement became filled with patients and hospital staff seeking shelter.

After three months of hospital treatment in Cologne and another three weeks in a military hospital in Bonn, Stewart was ready to be moved to his permanent prison camp, *Stalag Luft* 4D. It was there that he received his *Wartime Log* book from a Y.M.C.A. representative. Near the front of his book, neatly printed under the heading "Dedication," is the following:

> Out of everyone's life there are memories of things past that occupy a spot in our heart, a place never to be vacated.
> During my months as a P.O.W. I have made friends, dear friends, whose memory I shall hold in my thoughts throughout life. There is also a lighter side of this life which I shall often chuckle at in my idle hours.
> To these things I dedicate this book.

> *R.H.S.*

An American airman, minus a boot, parachutes to earth in this pencil sketch from Robert McVicker's *Wartime Log*. The explosion in the lower right corner was caused by the crash of the aircraft.

(COURTESY ROBERT MCVICKER)

One of the first pages in tail gunner Sylvan Cohen's *Wartime Log* features a montage in pencil that tells the story of his military service.

FOR YOU THE WAR IS OVER

STAMMLAGER LUFT I

" ABANDON HOPE ALL YE WHO ENTER HERE ! "

A watercolor perspective of the main gate at *Stalag Luft* I,
drawn by aviator Jack Friend in his *Wartime Log*. It shows the
large guard tower at the entrance and the German war flag
flapping in the wind on a summer day.

I would rather fly on 50 missions than go thru this again - We were 800 prisoners located on the target at Bolzano, Italy when the forts came!

The solitude of the *Stalag* 17 prison camp is captured in this rendering on a page of Sylvan Cohen's *Wartime Log.* The zigzag lines on the ground are trenches. In an air raid the prisoners were supposed to use the trenches as shelters.

(COURTESY HARDY Z. BOGUE III)

After prisoners were interrogated, they were assigned to a permanent prison camp and moved to that location in uncomfortable "forty-and-eight" railroad boxcars, designed to carry forty men or eight horses. The trip could cover hundreds of miles and last many days because the train often stopped to wait out Allied bombing raids or line repairs. Sometimes, the prisoners found themselves in the middle of an attack with nowhere to hide. Col. C. Ross Greening recalled the danger of one such episode in his *Wartime Log* with the hope that it would never happen again.

(COURTESY DOROTHY FISHBURNE)

Colonel Greening portrayed the arrival of new prisoners at the *Stalag Luft* I main gate on a cold, winter day. The new prisoners are carrying small suitcases known as "capture parcels" which were filled with clothing from the Red Cross. Funds for the supplies came from the Army Air Force. The wagon being pulled along the street between the barracks is filled with *Kriegsbrot*—German war bread—a prison food staple.

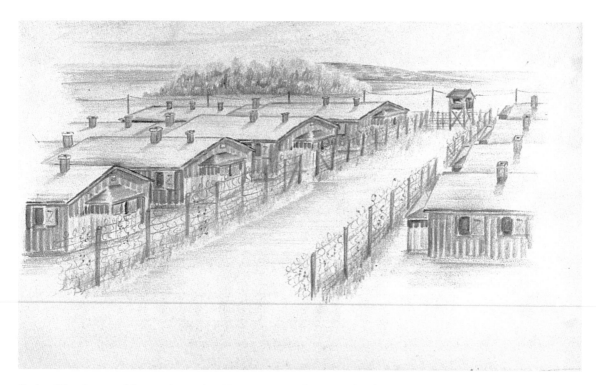

Stalag 17 prisoners' barracks and a German guard tower (in the distance) are shown in this view from Sylvan Cohen's log book. The two barbed wire fences separate one prison compound from another. The open area in the center was a virtual "no man's land." Airmen from different nations were segregated in this way later in the war, but during the war's early years, when there were far fewer prisoners, the men were mixed together.

(COURTESY HARDY Z. BOGUE III)

A typical guard tower at *Stalag Luft* III shows a searchlight mounted on the side and a machine gun pointed skyward. Weapons were normally not pictured in *Wartime Log* books out of fear of German authority, but prisoner Claudius Belk disregarded this custom.

(COURTESY NORM FLAYDERMAN)

POSITION OF STALAG LUFT I

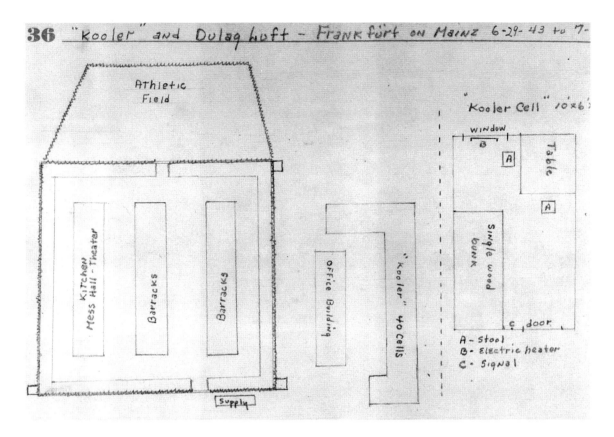

36 "Kooler" and Dulag Luft - Frankfurt on Mainz 6-29-43 to 7-

Athletic Field

Mess Hall - Theater / Kitchen

Barracks

Barracks

Office Building

"Kooler" 40 Cells

Supply

"Kooler Cell" 10'x6'

Window

Table

Single wood bunk

door

A - Stool
B - Electric heater
C - Signal

This detailed map, drawn by Claudius Belk, shows the *Dulag Luft* interrogation center near Frankfurt.

(COURTESY NORM FLAYDERMAN)

B-24 bombardier Jack Friend painted this unusual overhead view of *Stalag Luft* I prison camp in his log book. He included a number of nearby landmarks such as the flak school, the labor camp, and the airport with its assortment of vintage aircraft.

(COURTESY JACK FRIEND)

IF

If I hadn't had the notion I wanted silver wings,
If I hadn't let emotion blind my eyes to safer things,
If I only had been willing to instruct some other boys,
If I hadn't been so eager to get amid the noise,
If I hadn't been on schedule to fly that certain day,
If I'd only been more careful and kept out of the way,
If fate had only let me be free another night,
If I could have spoken German and said just what was right,
If I only quit my griping and realize just how
Very, very lucky, I am to be here now.

— FROM CLAUDIUS BELK'S *WARTIME LOG*
(COURTESY NORM FLAYDERMAN)

The boredom of prison camp life is depicted in this watercolor view of *Stalag Luft* I by Col. C. Ross Greening. Clothing dries on a line near the barbed wire fence and prisoners sunbathe or sit alone with their thoughts. Walking was a popular pastime and the walkway at right, just inside the wire separating two compounds, became a well-worn path.

original by

"I WANTED WINGS"!

~ A General Summary of a Day at Sagan for POW # 1670 ~

0845 : Get up
0900 : Breakfast
0930 : Morning Appelle
1030 -} Read, Study, Exercise
1200 } or visit
1200 : Noon Meal
1300 } Read, Study, wash
1600 } clothes, etc.
1620 : Main Meal
1645 : Afternoon Appelle
1700 } Bridge, study, reading
2400 } flapping, etc.
2115 : Half hour walk - brew
2145 : Tattoo
2200 : Taps - Lock-up

Afternoon appelle on Saturday and Sunday at 1600 - Morning appelle 1100 Sunday. Church Services: Protestant - Sunday 1100 with Vesper Service at 2000, Communion once a month, Bible Study Group 2000 Saturday. A General Service Non-Demoninational held in theatre by Padre Mc Donald. Special Services are held by Mormon and Christian Sc. Groups, and Regular Catholic Services are held by a POW Catholic Father. Music is played over the speaker system daily. Some time is spent of each day in preparing meals, washing dishes, etc. All include a "Kriegie" may spend a full day of useful work and Recreation if he wishes to so employ himself.

© Walt Disney Company

Walt Disney Studios created a special insignia for Americans imprisoned in *Stalag Luft* III, Sagan, Germany. The noted cartoon animator produced many such colorful devices for United States Army Air Force fighter and bomber squadrons and this design, showing an imprisoned Donald Duck, was developed, according to Disney archives, in October 1943. Two *Wartime Log* books that have been located contain prisoner-drawn variations of the Disney design. All three convey the same frustration of all prisoners. Lt. Claudius Belk's book also contained an account of his daily prison schedule.

I WANTED

THE SACK

This is the sack, the Kriegie's throne
The one thing that is all his own
Six feet in length and three feet wide
With an eight inch board it calls its side.
Seven pine slats, a front and a back
All go to make a Kriegie's sack.

A mattress filled with sticks of wood
About as hard as anything could.
Put two blankets and a sheet
Then pat them down nice and neat;
Lay the pillow at the head
Quick like a flash jump into bed
Stretch out your feet and lay way back
You're in heaven boy—you're on your sack.

— FROM JOHN HOWARD ADAMS'S *WARTIME LOG*
(COURTESY JOHN HOWARD ADAMS)

Well Dresse,
"Kriegie" of
1943

Clothing was often in short supply in the prisoner of war camps,
especially early in the war.
Prisoner Claudius Belk used
watercolors to document the
ragged and tattered look at *Stalag
Luft* III.

(COURTESY NORM FLAYDERMAN)

Edward Wodicka satirizes the "sack" in
this cartoon. The Germans provided
straw and a bag for a mattress which
rested on a wooden frame. After a few
uses the mattress became flattened and
was extremely uncomfortable.

(COURTESY EDWARD WODICKA)

NAME, RANK & SERIAL NUMBER

ON THE WALL IN A SOLITARY CONFINEMENT CELL

It's easy to be nice boys, when everything's okay
It's easy to be cheerful when you're having things your way
But can you hold your head up and take it on the chin
When your heart is nearly breaking and you'd like giving in.

It was easy back in England, amongst the friends and folks
But now you miss the friendly hand, the songs, the joys, the jokes
The road ahead is stony, and unless you're strong in mind
You'll find it isn't long before you're lagging far behind.

You've got to climb the hill boy, it's no use turning back
There's only one way home, and it's off the beaten track
Remember you're American, and when you reach the crest
You'll see a valley long and green—America at her best.

You know there is a saying that "sunshine follows rain"
And sure enough you'll realize that joy follows pain
Let courage be your password, make fortitude your guide
And then instead of grousing, just remember those that died.

— FROM SECOND LIEUTENANT ROY E. WENDELL, JR.'S *WARTIME LOG*,
STALAG LUFT I, BARTH, GERMANY. A B-17 NAVIGATOR,
HE WAS SHOT DOWN DURING A BOMBING MISSION OVER
FRANKFURT, GERMANY, 29 JANUARY 1944. IT WAS HIS THIRTEENTH MISSION.
(COURTESY ROY WENDELL)

According to Geneva Convention provisions captured fliers could be held for up to thirty days in the "cooler," one of many solitary confinement cells at the interrogation center near Frankfurt. B-24 bombardier Jack Friend recreated the solitary experience with this watercolor in his log book.
(COURTESY JACK FRIEND)

Nineteen-year-old Lieutenant Roy E. Wendell, Jr., who had grown up in Garden City, Long Island, not far from the beautiful Garden City Country Club and its manicured golf course, found himself in the not-so-picturesque environment of a German prison cell.

The cell was five feet wide and twelve feet long with an eight-foot-high ceiling. Within this austere setting were a cot and a table. Wendell remained in this solitary condition for about a week because, as he recalls almost fifty years later, "they just left you there."

The cell was one of many such rooms within the *Dulag Luft* interrogation center. The complex was located three hundred yards north of the main Frankfurt-Homburg road near the Kupforhammer trolley stop. Kupforhammer was the third trolley stop after Oberursel, thirteen kilometers northwest of Frankfurt.

Nearly all Air Force personnel captured in German-occupied Europe passed through the facility, which consisted of three components: the interrogation center at Oberursel, the hospital at Hohemark, and the transit camp, which was originally located in the Botanical Gardens of Frankfurt, but was later destroyed in Allied bombings. The new transit camp was a former German flak troop installation three kilometers from Wetzlar and fifty-three kilometers from Frankfurt.

By late 1943, about one thousand airmen were processed through the transit camp each month. This figure doubled in 1944. During the peak month—July 1944—three thousand Allied airmen and paratroopers passed through Wetzlar.

Captured airmen were usually placed in solitary confinement until the official interrogation began. This was part of the "softening-up" process employed by the Germans. Very little food was provided, there was no one to talk to; uncertainty prevailed.

Roy Wendell was captured soon after parachuting into an open field surrounded by German flak towers. While he sat in his cell, which was ice cold one moment, then unbearably hot the next, the small ceiling light was turned on and off periodically without reason. The airman made up

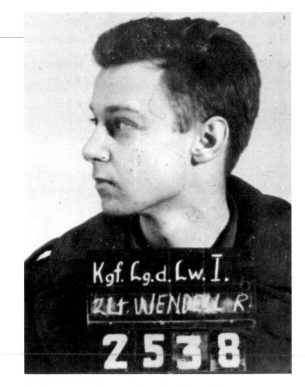

This photo shows Roy E. Wendell as a young prisoner of war. (COURTESY ROY E. WENDELL)

games to pass the hours. He even counted the number of nails in his tiny room. Within the confines of his mind he played baseball—anything to keep himself occupied.

"Then this guy came in and said he was from the Red Cross, which he wasn't," Wendell recalls. "Afterwards, I pounded on the door and said 'I want to talk.' Really, all I wanted to do was talk to someone. I had nothing to tell them, I just wanted to talk. I was wondering, what the hell is going on?"

Guards came and took him to a German officer, resplendent in a tailored uniform. The rank insignia on his shoulders indicated he was a major. It was early February, and it was cold—so cold the officer had placed his booted feet in a metal-lined wicker basket of warm coals.

"On one wall was a big map of England with a thumbtack at Ridgewell, home of my bomb group, the 381st," remembers Wendell. "There also was a mockup of a Norden bomb sight which was still secret. All this stuff to show you how much they already knew." The interrogation was about to begin.

(Continued)

Once taken prisoner, an airman usually received a "capture parcel" from the American Red Cross. It contained many of the items needed to begin life behind barbed wire.

(COURTESY AMERICAN RED CROSS)

American Red Cross "Capture Parcel" contains:

1	sweater	1	pair of pajamas	1	pair of bedroom slippers
1	tooth brush	2	pairs of socks	3	packages of razor blades
1	clothes brush	1	light undershirt	1	pair of light drawers
1	hair brush	1	tin of shoe polish	6	cakes of toilet soap
1	shoe cloth	1	box of cascara	2	bars of laundry soap
1	shaving stick	1	box of band-aids	1	tin of tooth powder
2	bath towels	2	pairs of shoe laces	1	package of pipe cleaners
2	face towels	1	box of vitamin tablets	3	packages of smoking tobacco
4	handkerchiefs	1	pocket comb and cover	1	"housewife" (containing
1	pipe	1	carton of cigarettes		needles, thread, buttons, pins,
1	safety razor	1	carton of chewing gum		safety pins, and darning cotton

All packed in a fibre suit case as shown in the picture.

"All I can give you is name, rank, and serial number," the navigator recalls telling his questioner. The German officer then proceeded to provide the American with information. First, Wendell's father's first name, his mother's maiden name, and where his parents had met and lived. Then he showed the American a copy of the official orders which had sent him to England. He also knew his bomb group and gave him a complete rundown on his group and aircraft.

"I just wondered," Wendell asks, "where did they get that kind of stuff?" Loose lips and spies, he thought.

"Before we pulled out on the *Queen Mary* to come over, when they shipped us from New Jersey to New York, we had to remove all signs that indicated that we were Air Force . . . wings, rank insignia, the 'wings and prop' pins, and the like," remembers Wendell. These precautions were taken to confuse spies.

The England-bound aviators, who numbered fifteen thousand according to Wendell, filed onto the *Queen Mary* in the darkness of the middle of the night.

"The next day, about eleven o'clock in the morning, we pulled out into the Hudson River with the band on the dock playing the Air Force song, while we were going down the Hudson River! A big secret!"

To each of the questions posed by the German major, the captive simply responded:

"Roy Wendell, 0-688146."

"Finally," Wendell explains, "I said, 'Look, if a German flyer gets shot down over England, he's not expected to give any more than I'm giving you. Name, rank, and serial number. I don't see how the hell you expect me to give you any more than that. And I'm not going to!'"

Anger filled the German officer's face. A sharp snapping noise startled the navigator.

"He broke a pencil," Wendell recalls, "jumped up and threw the pieces down on the table, and putting his finger in my face, said, 'Don't you dare compare yourself with a Luftwaffe flyer!'"

"Oh, no!" the concerned navigator thought to himself. "I said the wrong thing. I had to go and say the wrong thing! That did it."

A guard was summoned to remove Wendell from the room. Wendell was rushed back to his cell.

"I thought, what are they going to do now? Shoot? Put bamboo under the nails? But they didn't. That was the turning point. I guess they felt they had their shot at me and they would take the next one in line."

The next stop for the captured navigator was the prison camp at Barth, Germany—*Stalag Luft* I.

This cartoon from Richard H. Stewart's *Wartime Log* shows a captured airman being searched. "God in heaven!" the guard exclaims when he finds an escape device. "What's going on? What else is in the pockets?"

(COURTESY RICHARD H. STEWART)

Photos of the *Dulag Luft* mess hall show Americans waiting for fellow prisoners to arrive (above) and at mealtime (below).
(COURTESY AMERICAN RED CROSS)

A typical prisoners' room at *Stalag Luft* I is shown in this photograph taken in Barracks 3 of the South Compound. As many as sixteen men were crowded into these cramped sleeping quarters, which also served as a dining area and a laundry room.

(COURTESY JACK FRIEND)

CAGED BIRDMEN

During World War II 130,201 American servicemen were captured in Europe and the Pacific. Several thousand additional Army Air Force personnel were interned in neutral countries including Switzerland and Sweden.

Thirty-four thousand nine hundred four of them were Army Air Force personnel—both commissioned and noncommissioned officers—held in German prison camps.

According to Dr. Charles A. Stenger, a psychologist and consultant for the American Ex-Prisoners of War Association, 14,072 of the 130,201 prisoners died in captivity during World War II. Of that number, 2,759 were Army Air Force personnel. In the European and Mediterranean theaters, 202 died during captivity; 2,481 died in the Pacific and China-Burma-India prisons. Seventy-six P.O.W.s died in other theaters, en route to camps, or in unknown locations.

The War Department's Military Intelligence Service published two reports entitled "American Prisoners of War in Germany." The first was published during the war, on 15 July 1944, the second after the war, on 1 November 1945. (See Appendix for details.)

The first report states that as of mid-1944, Germany held a total of 8,447 Air Force officers and 8,146 Air Force enlisted men for a total of 16,593 Army Air Force personnel. These figures were compiled after the Normandy invasion. The 1945 War Department report states that there were 92,965 American prisoners of war held in Germany. Of these, 32,730 were Army Air Force personnel. (This figure is 2,174 less than the figure used by Dr. Stenger and the American Ex-Prisoners of War Association. Their figures are based on a government report published in 1953.)

Approximately 50 percent of the captured Air Force personnel were officers, while approximately 10 percent of ground force prisoners were officers.

The disparity between these two reports (16,593 prisoners versus 32,730 prisoners) can be attributed to the increase in bombing which occurred during that period of the war.

THE GENEVA CONVENTION

The ultimate fate of the prisoners depended on the treatment they received from their captors. The Geneva Convention was an attempt to standardize and improve the treatment prisoners received.

On 27 July 1929 forty-seven countries, including the United States and Germany, signed the "Convention Geneva Relative to the Treatment of Prisoners of War," the first formal codification of international law dealing solely with the treatment of prisoners of war. Ten international powers, including Japan, failed to ratify the agreement. Six of those ten nations later complied with the provisions. The Union of Soviet Socialist Republics never signed the document.

The basis for discussions at the conference was a draft text prepared by the International Committee of the Red Cross, which had been studying the prisoner of war question for eight years. The Red Cross would continue to be a dominant force in the lives of all World War II prisoners.

The convention contained eighty-two articles. Following are highlights of those articles that provided the greatest protection for prisoners of war.

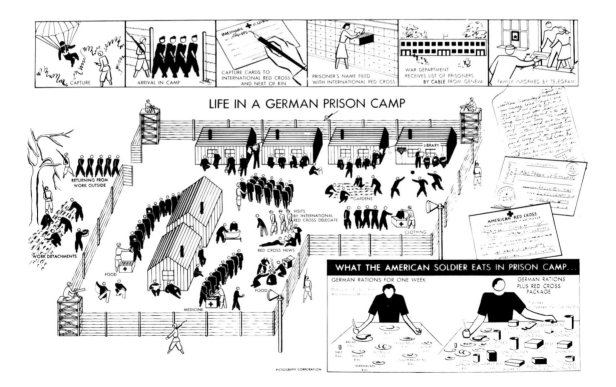

This American Red Cross drawing shows the treatment a captured airman could expect to receive. It appeared in the American Red Cross's *Prisoners of War Bulletin*, which was published for the relatives of American P.O.W.s and civilian internees.

(COURTESY AMERICAN RED CROSS)

Article 2—Prisoners of war are in the power of the hostile Power, but not of the individuals or corps who have captured them. They must at all times be humanely treated and protected, particularly against acts of violence, insults, and public curiosity. Measures of reprisal against them are prohibited . . .

Article 5—Every prisoner of war is bound to give, if he is questioned on the subject, his true name and rank, or else his regimental number. If he infringes this rule, he is liable to have the advantages given to prisoners of his class curtailed. No coercion may be used on prisoners to secure information relative to the condition of their army or country. Prisoners who refuse to answer may not be threatened, insulted, or exposed to unpleasant or disadvantageous treatment of any kind whatever . . .

Article 7—Prisoners of war shall be evacuated within the shortest possible period after their capture, to depots located in a region far enough from the zone of combat for them to be out of danger . . .

Article 10—Prisoners of war shall be lodged in buildings or in barracks affording all possible guarantees of hygiene and healthfulness. The quarters must be fully protected from dampness, sufficiently heated and lighted.

Article 11—The food ration of prisoners of war shall be equal in quantity and quality to that of troops at base camps. Furthermore, prisoners shall receive facilities for preparing, themselves, additional food which they might have. A sufficiency of potable water shall be furnished them.

Article 12—Clothing, linen and footwear shall be furnished prisoners of war by the detaining power. Replacement and repairing of these effects must be assured regularly . . .

Article 14—Every camp shall have an infirmary, where prisoners of war shall receive every kind of attention they need.

Article 15—Medical inspections of prisoners of war shall be arranged at least once a month . . .

Article 17—So far as possible, belligerents shall encourage intellectual diversions and sports organized by prisoners of war . . .

Article 27—Belligerents may utilize the labor of able prisoners of war, according to their rank and aptitude, officers and persons of equivalent status excepted. However, if officers or persons of equivalent status request suitable work, it shall be secured for them so far as is possible. Non-commissioned officers who are prisoners of war shall only be required to do supervisory work, unless they expressly request a remunerative occupation . . .

Article 36—Each of the belligerents shall periodically determine the number of letters and postal cards per month which prisoners of war of the various classes shall be allowed to send . . . Within a period of not more than one week after his arrival at the camp . . . every prisoner shall be enabled to write his family a postal card informing it of his capture and of the state of his health. The said postal cards shall be forwarded as rapidly as possible and may not be delayed in any manner . . .

Article 37—Prisoners of war shall be allowed individually to receive parcels by mail, containing foods and other articles intended to supply them with food or clothing. Packages shall be delivered to the addresses and a receipt given . . .

Article 39—Prisoners of war shall be allowed to receive shipments of books individually,

(Continued)

In accordance with article seventeen of the Geneva Convention, prisoners were allowed to attend classes and participate in athletic events. These photos, taken at *Stalag Luft* III, show airmen running in a track meet and studying in a math class.

(COURTESY AMERICAN RED CROSS)

which may be subject to censorship. Representatives of the protecting Powers and duly recognized and authorized aid societies may send books and collections of books to the libraries of prisoners' camps . . .

Article 43—In every place where there are prisoners of war, they shall be allowed to appoint agents entrusted with representing them directly with military authorities and protecting Powers. The agents shall be entrusted with the reception and distribution of collective shipments. In camps of officers and persons of equivalent status, the senior officer prisoner of the highest rank shall be recognized as intermediary between the camp authorities and the officers and persons of equivalent status who are prisoners . . .

Article 50—Escaped prisoners of war who are retaken before being able to rejoin their own army or to leave the territory occupied by the army which captured them shall be liable only to disciplinary punishment . . .

Article 54—Arrest is the most severe disciplinary punishment which may be imposed on a prisoner of war. The duration of a single punishment may not exceed thirty days . . .

Article 56—Prisoners punished shall be enabled to keep themselves in a state of cleanliness. These prisoners shall every day be allowed to exercise or to stay in the open air at least two hours . . .

Article 76—Belligerents shall see that prisoners of war dying in captivity are honorably buried and that the graves bear all due information, are respected and properly maintained . . .

Article 77—Each of the belligerent Powers . . . shall institute an official information bureau for prisoners of war who are within their territory. Within the shortest possible period, each of the belligerent Powers shall inform its information bureau of every capture of prisoners effected by its armies, giving it all the information regarding identity which it has, allowing it quickly to advise the families concerned, and informing it of the official addresses to which families may write to prisoners . . .

Article 78—Relief societies for prisoners of war, which are properly constituted in accordance with the laws of their country and with the object of serving as the channel for charitable effort, shall receive from the belligerents, for themselves and their duly accredited agents, every facility for the efficient performance of their humane task within the bounds imposed by military necessities. Agents of these societies may be admitted to the camps for the purpose of distributing relief . . .

Article 79—A central information agency for prisoners of war shall be created in a neutral country. The International Committee of the Red Cross shall propose the organization of such an agency to the interested Powers, if it considers it necessary. The function of that agency shall be to centralize all information respecting prisoners, which it may obtain through official or private channels; it shall transmit it as quickly as possible to the country of origin of the prisoners or to the Power which they have served.

Most of the time, the regulations concerning the prisoners' welfare were followed by German authorities. There were times, however, either due to the captors' unwillingness or to circumstances beyond their control, when the provisions of the Geneva Convention were not honored.

The International Committee of the Red Cross in Geneva, Switzerland, maintained massive files on the conditions of P.O.W.s. This information was made available to families of P.O.W.s and government officials.

(COURTESY AMERICAN RED CROSS)

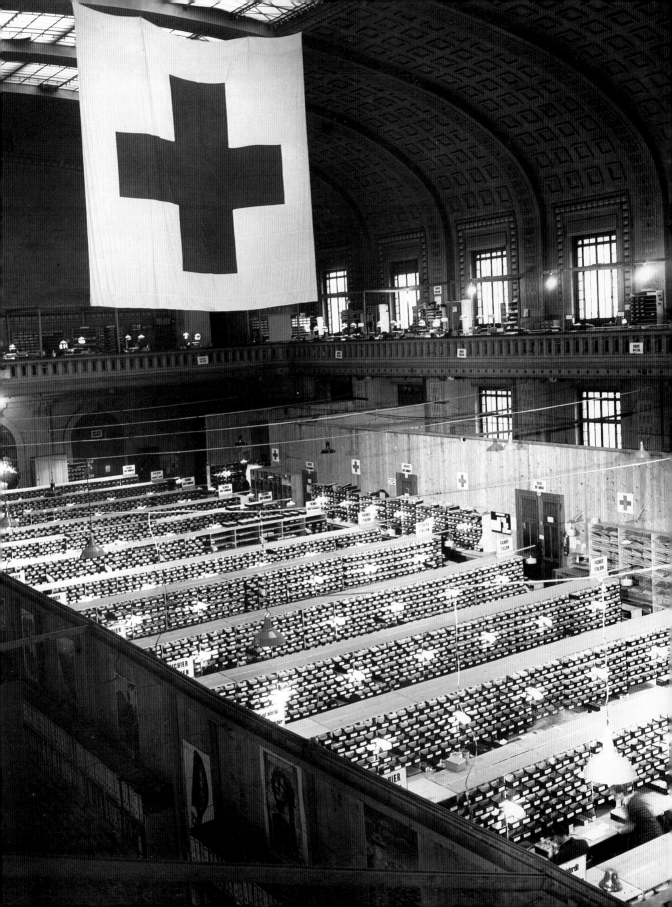

DEC 1 1 1944

WAR PRISONERS AID NEWS

YMCA

Published by
War Prisoners Aid of the Y.M.C.A.,
347 Madison Ave., New York 17, N. Y.

A participating service of the
NATIONAL WAR FUND.

Vol. 1   403   DECEMBER, 1944   No. 7

Christmas, 1944: I Was in Prison, and Ye Came unto Me

THE PRISONER

It's a melancholy state,
You are in the power of the enemy.
You owe your life to his humanity,
Your daily bread to his compassion.
You must obey his orders,
Await his pleasures,
Possess your soul to his patience.

The days are very long,
The hours crawl like paralyzed centipedes,
Moreover, the whole atmosphere of Prison,
—Even the most easy and best regulated Prison—
is "Odious."

Companions quarrel about trifles, and get the
Least possible pleasure from each other's society.
You feel a constant humiliation in being
Fenced in by railings and wire,
Watched by armed men and webbed about by
A triangle of regulation and restrictions.

— THOUGHTS ON BEING A PRISONER OF WAR BY WINSTON CHURCHILL,
WHO WAS CAPTURED IN 1899 DURING THE SOUTH AFRICAN WAR WHILE
SERVING AS A WAR CORRESPONDENT. FROM THE *WARTIME LOG* OF FIRST
LIEUTENANT JOHN HOWARD ADAMS. (COURTESY JOHN HOWARD ADAMS)

And in the same log:

Solitude was the most precious thing in the world if you knew how to employ it. It built up your endurance and permitted you to see yourself coldly, with all your faults and virtues; it allowed you to get some sort of perspective on things. It made it possible to face and to endure many things which otherwise would have been unendurable. If you suffered in solitude there was no need to parade your suffering shamefully in public . . .

. . . Now the immediate thing is to go on living, picking up the small threads. That alone will help the pain and bring back the knowledge that there is tragedy in life which we must endure and put it in its proper place in the scheme of things, into that perspective from which one will see it much later in life. In all things, in all human experience, even in tragedy there is a richness which must not be denied lest it turn into a cancer which devours you . . .

— LOUIS BROMFIELD, *MRS. PARKINGTON.*
(COURTESY JOHN HOWARD ADAMS)
REPRINTED WITH PERMISSION OF HARPERCOLLINS,
FROM *MRS. PARKINGTON*, BY LOUIS BROMFIELD. © 1943 BY HARPERCOLLINS.

The December 1944, edition of the *War Prisoners Aid News*, which was distributed by the Y.M.C.A. to relatives of American prisoners, featured this poignant cover.

(COURTESY YMCA OF
THE USA ARCHIVES,
UNIVERSITY OF MINNESOTA
LIBRARIES)

Large numbers of Army Air Force P.O.W.s escaped from their camps during World War II into their Y.M.C.A. *Wartime Log* books. The books provided a catharsis for the prisoners.

"In one way," former prisoner Roy Wendell says of his book, "it was a diary, and in another way the book was a form of escape. Here you are [in prison camp], you're sitting there, you don't know if you're going to get back at all. So you start thinking back to what you left behind. In a way it's an escape, an escape from the reality of the camp."

Wendell and other prisoners with log books spent hours writing and drawing. They sometimes swapped books in order to have another person provide a drawing of a different style. They also swapped cigarettes and other valuable commodites for artwork.

Much of the art had an untrained style, but some creations were crafted by prisoners who were professional artists. From a psychological view, working in the book provided a sense of accomplishment, according to Dr. Charles A. Stenger, a psychologist and former prisoner of war.

According to Dr. Stenger, when a prisoner is busy working, whether throwing coal in a furnace, filling bomb craters, or working in a log book, he is being productive and therefore earns a sense of accomplishment. But if the prisoner is inactive, he is continually reminded of his powerless situation. Depression inevitably results.

By working in the *Wartime Log*, the prisoner could escape from the harsh reality of the prison camp.

"When you are in that situation it's almost as if the other world no longer exists," Stenger explains. "You are totally involved in the current, the present world, because there's no way to escape from it. So this [working in the log] is a reminder that there really is another world."

Food was a major concern of the prisoner, and the log books often contained listings of favorite hometown restaurants, favorite entrees, and a menu for the first meal the prisoner wished to eat when he returned home.

"It's part of this escaping to pleasant thoughts about what might be possible in the future," Dr. Stenger adds. "A person is very conscious of the fact that it's a fantasy about what they would like the world to be like at the nearest opportunity. So it's part of the escape from the boredom and loneliness and all the other aspects of the prison life. It's a knowing escape, they're doing it consciously, knowing that thinking about these things is a lot better than focusing totally on what is immediately outside your head."

B-17 copilot Joseph Boyle drew a series of
cartoons depicting the first week of a new
prisoner's life in his *Wartime Log*.

(COURTESY JOSEPH BOYLE)

An ink-wash drawing from tail gunner Sylvan Cohen's *Wartime Log* shows the crowded barracks. One prisoner shaves while another mends clothing. A third plays solitaire and the fourth man rests in the upper bunk.

CAMP LIFE

Appel (roll call) was conducted by the Germans twice each day to determine if anyone had escaped. Col. C. Ross Greening documented the event in North Compound One at *Stalag Luft* I in this watercolor.

(COURTESY DOROTHY FISHBURNE AND BROWN & BIGELOW)

Four thousand meals were served daily to two thousand men in the communal mess hall of North Compound One in *Stalag Luft* I before the building burned to the ground. The meals were prepared from pooled Red Cross food parcels. Col. C. Ross Greening's watercolor shows prisoners filing into the mess hall that also served as a lecture hall, theater, schoolroom, and church.

(COURTESY DOROTHY FISHBURNE AND BROWN & BIGELOW)

GOOD NEW YORK BEANERYS

White Turkey Town House—Good layer cake and fowl; place to take the family; Washington Square & 5th Ave., 36th & Madison; Dinner $1.25.

Palms—46th & 2nd Ave.; John Ganz proprietor; Italian steaks; Hangout for News Cartoonists; Good Spaghetti; Dinner $1.75.

Oyster Bar—Grand Central; Sea Foods; Fruit Salad; Open all hours-Best 10 Sunday morning; Dinner $1.25, Breakfast $.75.

Brevoort—5th & 10th St; French; Best Onion Soup; Old N.Y. Atmosphere; Dinner $1.50.

Manny Wolfe's—3rd & 49th St; Steak House; Best Porterhouse with French Fries and Onions for $2.50; Dinner $1.50.

SMALL PLACES

Washington Irving House—17th and Irving Place—Old N.Y. Atmosphere—Best Omelets and Deep Dish Pies—Lunch $.50; Dinner $.75.

Diana's Coffee Shop—Very Small—Diana an Old Lady Running Business to Kill Time—Best Flank Steak—33rd E. of Lexington.

SNACKS

Ham 'n Eggery—Times Square—Eggs Cooked to Style and eaten Out of Pan—11 P.M. to 11 A.M.—Breakfast $.50.

(For Cheese Cake—79th, Right Side, 3 Doors off Broadway—Bakery)

— FROM ROY E. WENDELL'S *WARTIME LOG*
(COURTESY ROY E. WENDELL)

Food, according to Lt. Roy Wendell, was on everyone's mind, especially when there wasn't enough to go around. Aviator Wendell weighed 135 pounds when he entered the service but only 95 pounds by the time he was liberated from *Stalag Luft* I.

Coal rations for heating were often meager and B-17 navigator Edward Wodicka, a prisoner in *Stalag Luft* III, Sagan, Germany, used the duck which resembles Disney's Donald Duck character in his *Wartime Log* book to make a simple, yet forceful, statement. The artwork was done by using colored pencils.

(COURTESY EDWARD WODICKA. USED BY PERMISSION OF THE WALT DISNEY COMPANY)

If heating coal was available, a barracks' stove provided heat for prisoners when the temperature dropped. Flight engineer Richard Stewart's *Wartime Log* featured this view entitled *Winter Comfort*. Empty cans that once contained powdered milk were attached to each other and used as a stovepipe to connect the stove with the barracks' flue.

(COURTESY RICHARD H. STEWART)

"WINTER COMFORT"

B-R-R-R - NO COAL !

The latrine was one place where a prisoner could find a brief respite from the crowded conditions of most camps. This watercolor from P.O.W. Claudius Belk's *Wartime Log* was titled *Study Hall*.

(COURTESY NORM FLAYDERMAN)

Study Hall

Poss 1-26-45

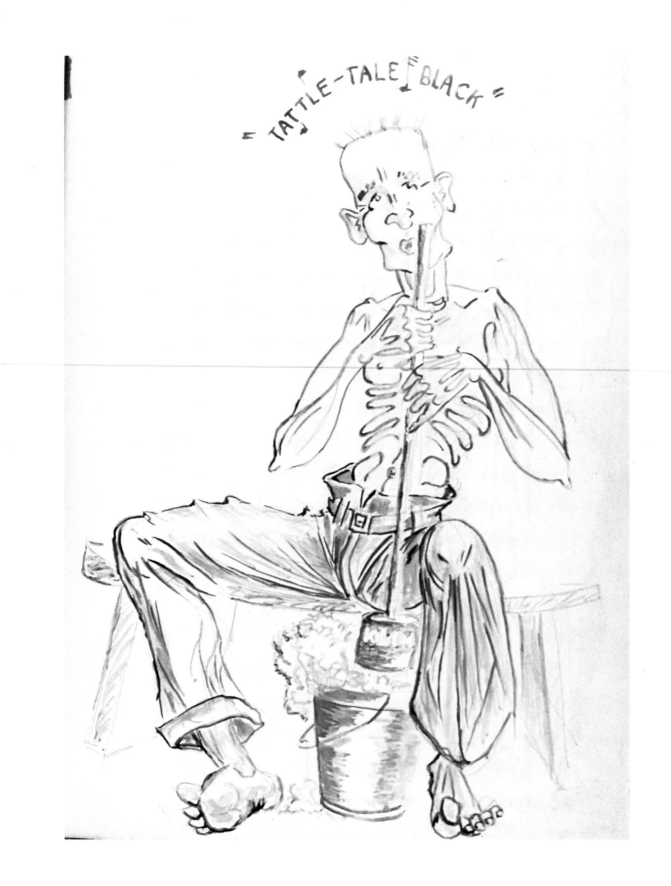

The prison barracks became a haven for lice and fleas, so prisoners laundered their clothing as often as possible to eliminate the unwanted guests. *Stalag Luft* III prisoner Claudius Belk devoted this watercolor cartoon to an airman about to clean the remnants of his clothes.

(COURTESY NORM FLAYDERMAN)

Kreige Washday

The prisoner's washing machine was a bucket of water and a stick attached to an empty food can. The agitating action depended on the prisoner's strength and patience. "Tattle-Tale-Black," according to Jack Friend, referred to the dirty condition of his clothing.

(COURTESY JACK FRIEND)

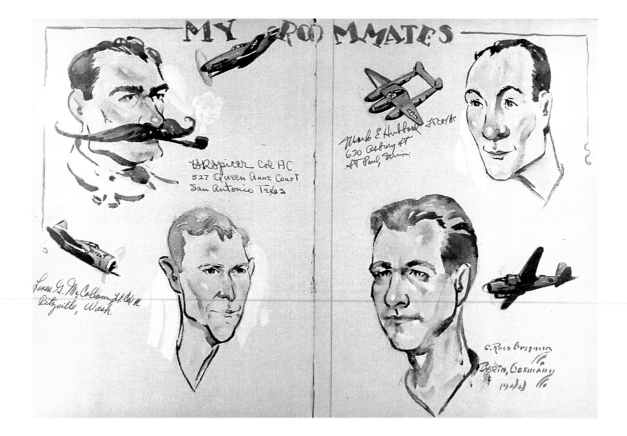

Lasting friendships were made in prison camp, especially among men who shared the same small room (with up to as many as fifteen other aviators). Col. C. Ross Greening placed this view of himself and three P.O.W. friends in his *Wartime Log.* It was also a common practice for prisoners to outline their American dog tags on pages of the book and then write the name and home address of fellow prisoners within the outlined shapes. Some books contain almost 100 such listings.

(COURTESY DOROTHY FISHBURNE)

**The reaction of a British aviator to American humor was depicted in this _Wartime Log_
watercolor cartoon by Lt. Edward Wodicka. The patched uniform was typical: prisoners
made do with whatever clothing they possessed.** (COURTESY EDWARD WODICKA)

Despite the protective Geneva Convention provisions, life in a prisoner of war camp could be dangerous—even deadly. One such *Stalag Luft* I occurrence was recorded by bombardier Jack Friend in this dramatic drawing that shows a pool of blood on the barracks floor. The incident occurred after an air raid alarm sounded. Camp regulations stipulated that all prisoners were to remain inside the building until the "all-clear" signal was given. One American aviator, however, did not hear the first alarm and opened the door to go outside. A guard in a distant tower noticed the movement and shot the prisoner where he stood.

(COURTESY JACK FRIEND)

B-17 copilot Joseph Boyle was a prolific cartoonist and poet while at *Stalag Luft* III. In his *Wartime Log* he painted this comic watercolor of the 4 July 1943 celebration initiated by a ride around the grounds by a Paul Revere impersonator who warned, "The British are coming!"

(COURTESY JOSEPH BOYLE)

July 4th
1943

Kriegie Celebration

Chess was a favorite activity, sure to consume many hours. Col. C. Ross Greening used two of his roommates to describe the "action" in his log book. He included cobwebs in the scene to highlight the pace of the game.

(COURTESY DOROTHY FISHBURNE)

At "Stalag One" we often whiled away a quiet evening at cards.

Card games, especially bridge, were popular with prisoners. Card tournaments were by necessity time-consuming and sometimes heated. Colonel Greening's *Wartime Log* contains his artistic interpretation of the pastime's competitive and combative nature.

(COURTESY DOROTHY FISHBURNE)

Why its hell to be a P.O.W.

"THAT'S WENDELL — JUST RETURNED FROM A P.O.W. CAMP!"

SACK TIME

Prisoner Roy E. Wendell placed the cartoon above in his book in anticipation of his liberation from *Stalag Luft* I. It summed up the thoughts most of the men held for months— even years—behind barbed wire.

(COURTESY ROY E. WENDELL)

Nightfall meant "sacktime," a time when prisoners hoped to lose themselves in dreams of home and more pleasant times. Navigator Edward Wodicka used one page of his *Wartime Log* to create this wine, women, and song theme.

(COURTESY EDWARD WODICKA)

Wartime Logs often contained paintings and drawings that focused on how much the prisoners missed women. Col. C. Ross Greening noted his hapless state in this watercolor at far left.

(COURTESY DOROTHY FISHBURNE)

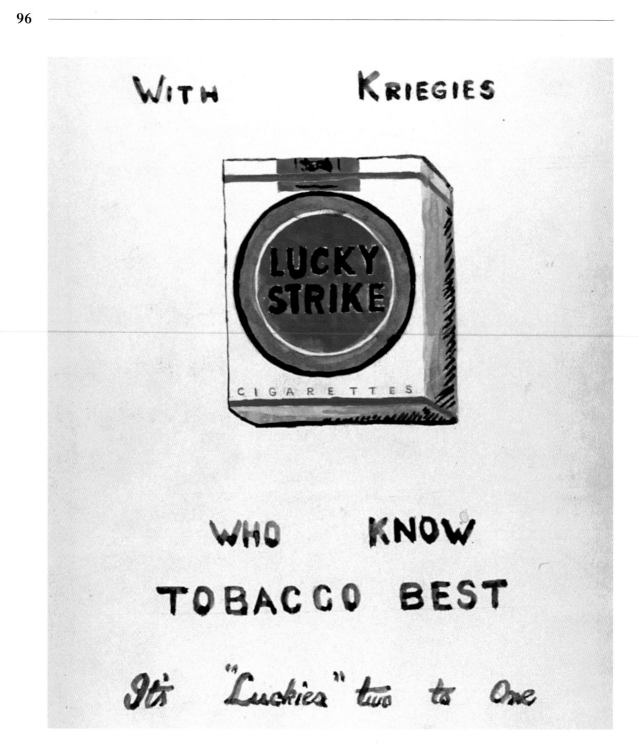

Tobacco products became an important part of every prisoner's life, even if he did not smoke. Cigarettes, cigars, and pipe tobacco were used in trades with fellow prisoners as well as with German guards. B-17 flight engineer Richard H. Stewart devoted a page of his log book to this valuable *Kriegie* asset.

(COURTESY RICHARD H. STEWART)

FOOD FOR THOUGHT

LOAVES OF BREAD (BLACK)

Hard and woody, coarse and rough,
Mealy, cracked, hard baked stuff.
Tough and sour, doughy and damp,
The heaviest food in the whole darn camp.

Slice it thin, slice it thick,
They say it's food—we shouldn't kick.
When we build a house on the old homestead,
We'll use it for bricks—this German bread!

— BY P.O.W. EARL MARTIN AS RECORDED
IN THE *WARTIME LOG* OF SECOND LIEUTENANT
EDWARD S. WODICKA, *STALAG LUFT* III.
(COURTESY EDWARD WODICKA)

The subject of food was of primary importance for Americans held captive in German prison camps.

The Germans were required by the provisions of the Geneva Convention to provide food to prisoners in the same quantity and quality as the food received by German troops (see Article 11, page 72). Army Air Force prisoners who had *Wartime Log* books often devoted a page to recording the basic, and mostly inadequate, staples they received.

Red Cross food parcels included cigarettes, which could be used as currency in trades with other prisoners or German guards.

(COURTESY AMERICAN RED CROSS)

Edward Wodicka, imprisoned in *Stalag Luft* III, Sagan, Germany, titled one page of his book "Reich Rations—If Received." The word "if" was underlined for emphasis.

Wodicka listed the weekly staples of bread, sugar, margarine, ersatz jam, cheese, and potatoes, as well as fresh meat ("every two weeks"), sausage ("sometimes"), and barley ("off and on"). Provision of these items to prisoners varied from camp to camp as did the quality of the food. A number of *Wartime Log* books noted that the quantity was not sufficient to maintain the health of the prisoners. One prisoner calculated that the food provided by the Germans amounted to six thousand grams per week, for a total 13.1 pounds per week, or 1.8 pounds of food per day.

"The meal amounts to one stew each day and about one breakfast per week," he wrote.

(Continued)

In the latter months of the war, the quantity of these meager rations was often reduced because the stepped-up Allied bombings of the German transportation system disrupted the shipment of food supplies to the camp.

Back home in the United States, the American Red Cross recognized that this diet was not sufficient. They developed a plan to provide supplementary food for each captive in the form of a "standard food package." Each package contained foods of the highest nutritive value. It was intended that each American prisoner would receive one package per week while in captivity. The American Red Cross paid the administrative costs of the program and each American service branch supplied funds to purchase the food parcels and pay the transportation costs.

In *Stalag Luft* I, navigator Roy Wendell devoted two full pages in his *Wartime Log* to an inventory of the items in the American, British, and Canadian parcels. The standard food package, Wendell recorded, contained cube sugar (eight ounces), cheese (eight ounces), jam or peanut butter (six ounces), crackers or cereal (seven ounces), a chocolate bar (eight or sixteen ounces), meat pâté (eight ounces), coffee (four ounces), margarine (eight to sixteen ounces), corned beef or C-ration (sixteen ounces), Spam (twelve ounces), prunes or raisins (sixteen ounces), powdered milk, also known as KLIM (sixteen ounces), salmon or tuna (eight ounces), soap (two bars), and cigarettes (five to seven packs). In addition to the standard package, the Red Cross assembled a special food and gift parcel for Christmas delivery, and developed an even more nutritious "invalid food package" for those prisoners recuperating from wounds.

The Red Cross opened three major food parcel packaging plants—in Philadelphia, Chicago, and New York—for the assembly of the food packages. Production was expected to reach 300,000 food packages per month, but during the first year of operation the monthly average was more than 650,000 packages. The plants were staffed by volunteers. Eventually, other plants were opened to supplement the effort, and by war's end food packages distributed to Americans

Volunteers at a Philadelphia Red Cross packing center assemble food parcels in March 1943 for American and Allied prisoners of war.

(COURTESY AMERICAN RED CROSS)

amounted to approximately twenty-two thousand tons or 3,219,885 individual food packages.

Arthur Robinson's *The History of the American National Red Cross,* published in 1950, reported that democracy ruled the volunteer force of workers at the Red Cross packaging plants. Millionaires worked next to those of modest means on the assembly line. Workers were not restricted by an age limit. A woman in her seventies who worked in the Philadelphia plant typified the volunteer spirit.

Her first job was putting packs of cigarettes into the standard food package. She worked a two-and-a-half-hour shift, three days a week, as did all assembly line volunteers. A ten-minute break split each shift in half.

After packing cigarettes for two weeks, the elderly volunteer asked her supervisor for permission to put containers of milk, the heaviest item, into the boxes. Her son, she explained, was a prisoner of war and did not smoke. He was, she said, very fond of milk and she hoped that one of the milk cans she packed would reach her boy. Permission was granted and the volunteer enthusiastically worked at her new assembly line post, packing two thousand milk containers weighing a total of one ton each day.

Once assembled the packages were moved to American ports for shipment on vessels owned or

(Continued)

Mountains of crates containing Red Cross food parcels were stored in huge warehouses in Geneva, Switzerland. Once the food parcels were unpacked, the crates they had been shipped in were used in the construction of camp chapels, theaters, classrooms, and seats. Nothing went to waste. (COURTESY AMERICAN RED CROSS)

leased by the Foundation for the Organization of Red Cross Transports, a subsidiary of the International Committee of the Red Cross. By the end of the war the foundation had transported American Red Cross supplies on all three vessels it owned—the *Caritas I, Caritas II,* and *Henry Dunant.* Three other ships—the *Mangalore, Travancore,* and *Saivo*—were operated under long-term charters. The organization also used eight chartered trips on other vessels to carry American Red Cross supplies to prisoners of war.

The Foundation ships traveled under Allied and Axis safe-conduct along routes that were approved in advance. At night they traveled fully lighted. Their sides were painted with "C. Internationale" and a large red cross. Crosses were also painted on the decks to identify the ships' status when viewed from the air. The route from U.S. ports took the vessels directly to Marseilles, France, or Genoa, Italy. A northern route was used later in the war when transportation in southern Europe was disrupted.

From these points the supplies were shipped by the International Committee of the Red Cross to Geneva, Switzerland, where they were warehoused in huge storage buildings, the stockpiles of boxes almost reaching the roof braces. It was the responsibility of the German government to move the goods from the border into the prison camps. Railroad locomotives and boxcars were

the primary means of transportation. After a long journey desperately needed food began to move into the camps.

The hunger returned in late 1944 and the first months of 1945 as Allied bombing raids systematically destroyed the German transportation facilities. Roads, bridges, and rail lines crumbled under the Allied attacks, and the prisoners received fewer and less frequent shipments of Red Cross parcels. In some cases stockpiles of parcels remained in warehouses because German officials prevented their distribution.

The seriousness of the situation became paramount in February 1945. In his Red Cross history, Robinson relates that in February, four grim-faced representatives of the International Committee of the Red Cross, including the chief of the delegation in Germany, met in Geneva with Dr. Carl Buckhardt, International Committee president. Their purpose was to give an eyewitness account of the incredible confusion in eastern Europe.

With a large map of Germany before them, they described the confusion from which they had come. More than 250,000 Allied prisoners of war, including Americans once held in eastern camps, a half-million slave laborers, more than one million German troops, and seven to eight million civilians were fleeing the advance of the Soviet military. In a state of utter confusion, with no food,

Drawings of Red Cross food parcels or shipping boxes were included in almost every *Wartime Log.* **The drawing to the left, from gunner Sylvan Cohen's book, shows packages stored on the bottom level of a bunk. Navigator Edward Wodicka drew a large Red Cross shipping crate next to the stove.** (COURTESY HARDY Z. BOGUE III AND EDWARD WODICKA)

water, shelter, or medical care, this sea of humanity trudged day and night, knee-deep in snow, in below-zero temperatures. Many paused to rest from their exhaustion only to freeze to death.

Some prisoners were able to take a bit of food with them when they were moved by the Germans from their camps. Surprisingly, a good number carried the *Wartime Log* books on their journey, despite the added weight. Some books were lost forever as prisoners tore pages from the personal histories and fed them into open fires along the route. Everything became fuel for a bit of added warmth.

The German ration for the prisoners and their accompanying guards was no more than one or two small (and often half-rotten) potatoes cooked into a thin soup. Those who had cans of corned beef or Spam found the contents frozen solid. They had to chip bits of food out of the cans and thaw the morsels in their mouths. It was estimated that forty percent of those on the march had frozen feet or hands. Sixty percent had dysentery. Their condition was desperate.

With rail transportation almost nonexistent and road transportation limited, U.S. Army trucks and Swiss block trains became the mode of transportation for relief supplies.

An emergency plan was developed to send a block train of fifty freight cars loaded with five hundred tons of food from Geneva to a subdepot at Moosburg, Germany, northeast of Munich. At that point the supplies were loaded into two-and-a-half-ton capacity American trucks. The trucks moved out and distributed the supplies. Each truck was protected with a large red cross painted on its roof and rear.

At a warehouse yard in Geneva, Henry Wasmer, the director of the International Committee of the Red Cross Relief Division, called together the sixty drivers, mechanics, and special agents who would accompany the convoy. Robinson's Red Cross history records that fateful gathering.

"We have informed the Allied air forces of the composition, the routes and the schedules of these convoys," Wasmer reportedly advised. "But we do not know whether this experiment will

MY RED CROSS BOX

I don't want to go home to-day
'Cause my little Red Cross box is due.
Take all my buddies, my blankets away
My pipe and barley stew
My tin cup and rusty knife,
My straw and extra pair of sox.
You can even take twenty-five years of my life
But give me my "Red Cross Box."

For it's Christmas time when the box rolls in
And my "guts" begin to shout
Just a little heaven of cardboard and tin,
But I'm really "sweating it out."
And I don't know what I'll do some day
When they open the rusty locks,
And make me go home, so far away
From my beautiful "Red Cross Box."

— FROM EDWARD WODICKA'S WARTIME LOG
(COURTESY EDWARD WODICKA)

work. The Committee has taken out life insurance on every man who goes into Germany, and every man who goes must be ready to be killed."

Then, one further admonition from Wasmer: "We consider this trip little short of suicidal and the only excuse for your making it is that you will help save thousands of men from suffering and from starvation. If any man wants to drop out, he can be sure no one will blame him, but this is your last chance."

The rail lines around Munich were under constant bombardment, so the American Red Cross delegate in Switzerland contacted the Allied Air Force headquarters to enable the supply train to reach the trucks at the Moosburg subdepot. Headquarters called off the bombers and the Germans, also desperate for safe transportation, quickly repaired the damaged Munich lines. After the tracks were repaired, the Red Cross train successfully made the run to Moosburg. Allied Air Force bombers and fighters followed the train and, once again, bombed and strafed the lines.

During the next day and a half, while the supplies were moved from the boxcars into the relief trucks at Moosburg, the bombing was again suspended so the Germans could repair the line. When the task was accomplished, the Red Cross train was able to return to Switzerland. Once the area was clear, Allied aircraft again destroyed the rail lines.

The truck convoy's mission was a success; it returned safely, having been guarded by numerous aircraft. Not one shot had been fired at the convoy and the new distribution system had been successful: some food had reached those on the march.

There wasn't much to laugh about when food was scarce in the prison camps. Nevertheless, flight engineer Richard H. Stewart was able to find humor in the situation. The standard food parcel was designed to feed one man each week, but a dearth of supply meant the men had to carefully ration the food.

(COURTESY RICHARD H. STEWART)

KRIEGIE RECIPES

Prisoners developed special recipes to enhance the taste of their meals and remind them of home. Sometimes they recorded the recipes in their *Wartime Log* books.

The following recipes, designed to feed twelve men, are from James Mankie's soft-covered log book:

CREAM CUSTARD PIE—Crust made of crackers or cereal (1 box of either). Have crust baked in sardine tins. Filling-1-1/2 can of cheese, 1-1/2 T/S oleo, 6 T/S sugar, add KLIM as needed. Melt cheese, oleo and sugar in three KLIM cans with enough water to cover ingredients. When melted stir with spinner to insure smooth mixture. Add KLIM and mix until fairly thick. Pour into crust and allow to set at least 4 hours.

SUGAR SNAPS—2 boxes of crackers, 8 T/S oleo, 22 level T/S of KLIM, 1-1/2 cups of sugar, 1/2 T/S of salt. Stir KLIM, crackers, salt and sugar. Dry. Add melted oleo, add water until batter is sticky. Set at least 1-1/2 hours. Drop from spoon and bake.

PRUNE WHIP—1-1/2 boxes of prunes, 1/2 can of KLIM (mixed thick), 1 box of cereal or crackers, 3 T/S of sugar. Stew prunes with sugar. When ready add KLIM and crackers. Beat well while cooking.

JELLY ROLLS—1-1/2 boxes of crackers, 4 T/S of sugar, 1/4 T/S salt, 1 T/S oleo, jam (as much as desired). Mix crackers, sugar and salt dry. Add melted oleo and enough KLIM paste to thin sufficiently. Roll out dough and cut into strips. Spread with jam. Roll and sprinkle with sugar. If necessary thicken jam with dry KLIM.

The *Wartime Log* of Daniel D. Wilkerson, Jr. contained the following recipes:

CHOCOLATE PIE—Box of "K2" crackers mixed with butter and water for crust. Mold into container and set up or heat to dry out. Mix one grated D-bar with butter, milk & water for filling. Beat to creamy paste and pour into crust. Then take powdered milk and mix with water, butter and sugar for icing. Beat well and add to pie. When pie is cold it slices neatly.

MEAT LOAF—Take "Gerry" potato ration and mash. Add milk if desirable. Two cans of salmon mixed with spuds. Mix well and add two slices grated "Gerry" bread. Pour into baking pan and grate one "K2" over top. Place slices of cheese on top and bake.

FUDGE—Grate one D-bar. Add one lb. sugar and small amt. of butter and set on hot fire. Stir well while cooking until small ball forms in cold water. Take off fire and heat well until stiff. Pour into greased pan and set to cool. Cut in squares and serve.

And from the *Wartime Log* of Patrick Reams:

FUDGE CAKE—1 D-bar, 1/4 lb. sugar, 2 tablespoons margarine, 1 cup KLIM, 1 box K-ration crackers, pinch salt. Crush crackers. Boil everything else to fudge consistency. Add crackers, stirring vigorously. Bake in cake pan until good crust forms.

The Red Cross prepared a special Christmas parcel for prisoners in 1944. Small gifts, including a pipe, a washcloth, and a print of a nineteenth century baseball game, were packed with the usual provisions. (COURTESY AMERICAN RED CROSS)

CHEESE SPREAD—1/2 lb. cheese, 1/2 lb. margarine, 1 cup KLIM, pinch of salt. Slice cheese. Add salt and margarine and start heating. As they melt, add KLIM. When cheese is dissolved, pâté bouillon cubes, etc., can be added to taste. Boil to thick cream consistency and allow to cool.

Copilot Reams concluded his recipe section with the following cooking hints which were necessitated by prison camp conditions:

1. All measurements are guesswork.
2. One teaspoon Red Cross tooth powder added to cake batter makes it rise a little and gives a ginger flavor.
3. To increase the amount of stew available, just add more water.

WANTED: A *WARTIME LOG*

Philadelphia native Edward S. Wodicka spent several months in a number of German hospitals recovering from wounds. The B-17 navigator was blown out of his disabled aircraft after incendiary ammunition from an enemy Focke-Wulf fighter ignited the bomber's payload. A German doctor removed a steel bomb fragment from Wodicka's leg. The operation, Wodicka was later told, saved his life. However, he suffered the effects of a broken elbow, an injury that was left to heal on its own.

When he entered his permanent prison camp, *Stalag Luft* III, at Sagan, Germany, Wodicka received a newcomer's special treatment to determine if he was indeed an American, and not a German plant. Plants were sometimes used to obtain potentially useful military information.

"The prisoners in the camp interrogated me," Wodicka remembers, and "found out where I was born and where I lived.

"They readily found someone that also lived in Philadelphia to interrogate me," the navigator recalls. "They wanted to determine whether or not I was a German stooge. But with the background I had this chap knew that I was a bona fide American prisoner of war." Wodicka said that the prisoners knew there were Germans who had lived in America prior to the war and learned to use American slang and mannerisms.

"That's why we were as careful as possible," he explained. "And that's why the prisoners there [already in camp] would interrogate any new, incoming prisoner. If a man didn't seem to have enough of a background, he was suspect. And he was shunned."

Wodicka had always been interested in art and took an immediate interest in the Y.M.C.A. *Wartime Log* books. He had not received a log book upon his arrival at *Stalag Luft* III, but he learned that some fellow airmen were not using their *Wartime Log* books. Armed with a number of chocolate D-bars, which served as a form of camp currency, Wodicka negotiated a trade. The book's original recipient got five D-bars.

Navigator Edward Wodicka, shown in his high-altitude insulated flight jacket, became a master at drawing portraits of fellow prisoners at *Stalag Luft* III. The pencil sketches from his *Wartime Log* captured the mood of prison camp life: not one man is shown smiling.

(COURTESY EDWARD WODICKA)

Wodicka got the log, which played an important role in his life while at Sagan.

"I wanted it because sketching was a hobby of mine and it would give me something to do," the artist explains. Other prisoners were using the books to record poetry, quotations, and drawings of camp life as well as stories of how other airmen had become prisoners.

"As soon as I could, I persuaded some of my fellow prisoners to sit for me so I could do their portraits," Wodicka says. The sittings usually took

(Continued)

about two hours. The result—some of the finest pencil sketches found in any of the *Wartime Log* books located.

P.O.W.s had to be careful with their subject matter, especially if it involved military topics. Twice each day, in the morning and early in the evening, the prisoners were required to fall into formation for *appel* (roll call). The Germans wanted to make sure no one had escaped.

During this time, which lasted anywhere from thirty minutes to several hours, the log books were left in the barracks. German camp officials checked the books for offensive content and useful information.

"I had been warned not to put anything in the log book that might seem offensive to them," Wodicka explains. "I did try to be careful in that regard. I do have a picture of a guard tower but I don't show any evidence of machine guns. Merely a spotlight."

Prisoner Roy Wendell reported that some American prisoners served as censors, periodically checking the log books for sensitive material. According to Wendell, if the censors discovered anything offensive, they tore it from the book and destroyed it.

The Y.M.C.A. *Wartime Log* became Wodicka's prized possession, and he tried to keep the book with him at all times. He made a knapsack out of clothing scraps and when he and the other prisoners were moved from the Sagan camp near the end of the war, his book was the first item in the bag.

"I wanted some memento of the service," he explains. "At that time it seemed to be most valuable. I had nothing else, you see."

All he owned were the clothes on his back, whatever food he could carry, and his precious log book.

THE ART OF LIVING

The barracks were alive with activity as colored crepe paper and the printed labels from Red Cross food cans were boiled so that colored liquid could be extracted and used as paint. Officers processed tree twigs into charcoal for sketching by baking the sticks. The art program at *Stalag Luft* I was in full swing.

By drawing and sketching, prisoners could record the events that led to their capture. Reminiscing about home brought the people and places dearest to them into their barracks. The harsh reality of the camp also provided subject matter. These experiences were transferred onto whatever paper was available. Many prisoners accepted their fate with a positive attitude that enabled them to find humor in their environment. This too was recorded with paint and pencil.

Paper was a scarce commodity in all of the camps. At first, scraps of whatever was available had to be used, including the wrapping from cigarette packs and toilet paper.

In 1943, the World Alliance of the Y.M.C.A. initiated a program to produce the blank, hard-covered *Wartime Log* books for the use of prisoners held by the Germans.

The books were delivered to the camps by Red Cross and Y.M.C.A. officials. Most of the *Wartime Log* books were distributed into the camps holding Air Force prisoners, probably because they were among the first American military personnel captured. Later, as the war progressed, transportation became more and more disrupted due to the continual bombing of rail lines, roads, and bridges. P.O.W.s were less likely to receive shipments of *Wartime Log* books (or anything else) during this time.

John R. Burkhart, associate director for the Y.M.C.A. War Prisoners Aid program, was made aware of the problems faced by the prisoners by reports from Y.M.C.A. field representatives who personally inspected the camps and by correspondence he received from prisoners. As liaison between American prisoners held in Germany and Italy and their families in America, he helped raise sixteen million dollars which was used to send recreational equipment, musical instruments, theatrical supplies, religious materials, and millions of books into the camps for prisoner use.

One day he received a letter from an Air Force pilot, Lt. Col. Charles Ross Greening, who had been shot down while leading a bombing mission against a German airfield at Naples, Italy. It was the second time he had to use his parachute—the first being in 1942 following the Doolittle Raid over Tokyo, when he was forced to bail out over China. After returning safely he requested combat duty again and became a group commander of a B-26 unit operating in North Africa. On 17 July 1943 he bailed out the second time and landed on the side of Mt. Vesuvius, where he was immediately captured. After two months of imprisonment he escaped, only to be recaptured six months later. He was then moved to *Stalag Luft* I.

Colonel Greening graduated with a fine arts degree from Washington State College in 1936.

Col. C. Ross Greening describes prisoner of war camp conditions. This photo was taken during the "Army Air Force P.O.W. Exposition" tour.

(COURTESY DOROTHY FISHBURNE)

This photo, taken in *Stalag Luft* I, shows prisoners waiting in line to view the "Kriegie Kraft Karnival" held in North Compound One's American mess hall 24-26 July 1944. (COURTESY DOROTHY FISHBURNE)

Painting came naturally to him and he enjoyed working in a variety of media. Behind the barbed wire of the *Stalag Luft* I prison camp, the pilot used ingenuity to obtain many of the materials needed for his work.

Methods such as soaking and boiling were devised to produce watercolors from ersatz coffee grounds, printed labels, and other available colored paper. Bright red German coal dust was used as a paint base and prisoners traded cigarettes with German guards for colored pencils, which were then dissolved in water to provide additional color for painting. Human hair was used in the fabrication of paint brushes. Lead pencils, which are ideal for sketching, were in very short supply. The Germans provided a small allowance of pencils for use in the camp and more were acquired in trades with guards.

"These pencils were overworked to the point that little holders were devised from tin cans to utilize the last particle of lead," Greening wrote after the war.

Prisoners interested in sculpture needed tools.

German stoves were dismantled to provide iron bars that could be heated and pounded into the desired cutting tools. The tools were finely sharpened on rocks and bricks that had been found in camp.

According to Burkhart, Greening's letter was a request for more traditional art supplies, not only for himself, but for the rest of the camp.

Arrangements were made to acquire and ship the material to Germany and Greening received the supplies.

The Allied prisoners continued to follow the chain of command and discipline in the camps. Because of his rank, when Greening arrived at *Stalag Luft* I he became commanding officer of North Compound One. Command was assigned according to rank, from the commanding officer of an entire camp all the way down to the man in charge of an individual room, which housed up to sixteen men.

Besides the duties he assumed in his compound position, Colonel Greening felt he could also serve his fellow prisoners in another way. While some prisoners at *Stalag Luft* I had been involved with arts and crafts before the colonel's arrival, Greening organized classes so that he could share his knowledge of art with as many "students" as possible.

His widow, Dorothy Fishburne, says that her husband "had to be doing something all the time, and it was usually artwork." When Colonel Greening got to *Stalag Luft* I, according to his widow, he found some of the prisoners had nothing to do. They had become despondent.

"I think he just felt impelled to get them motivated," she explains.

The art program grew in popularity as Y.M.C.A. art supplies, *Wartime Log* books, and smaller, soft-covered booklets became available.

Greening later wrote that he had "never seen so many artists at work in [his] life. Everybody [was] engaged in some sort of activity that provided the release of energy denied through confinement."

The art program was so successful that Colonel Greening staged an exhibit called the "Kriegie Kraft Karnival" in the American camp mess hall from 24-26 July 1944. The term *Kriegie* was prisoner slang for the German word *Kriegsgefangenen*, meaning prisoner of war.

A seemingly endless line of prisoners patiently waited in line to view the exhibit. Once inside, they inspected hundreds of pieces of artwork, including paintings, drawings, cartoons, model airplanes, sculpture, handmade cooking utensils, and plaques. The plaques were decorated with wings and other insignia made from lead salvaged from Red Cross food cans and metal from empty toothpaste tubes. The hit of the show was a full-size violin made from bed slats and a table leg.

After the war the exhibit was shown throughout the United States as part of a national tour organized by Colonel Greening. His paintings of aerial combat, camp scenes, and personalities were later published in a book entitled *Not as Briefed*. The Y.M.C.A. thought so much of his efforts on behalf of his fellow prisoners that the organization awarded Colonel Greening its "Flame of Freedom" medal.

ART STUDENTS

Fighter pilot Al Ricci was shot down on 16 March 1944 while flying his P-51 Mustang as element leader on his fourteenth mission. When Ricci's element broke through the thick clouds at twenty-five thousand feet, they found themselves behind a flight of four Messerschmitt 109 fighters. The Me-109 pilots dove to the left.

As Ricci followed the German aircraft he tried to jettison the extra fuel tanks located on each wing of his aircraft. Although the tanks gave the plane greater flying range, they were a detriment in aerial combat because they made the aircraft less maneuverable.

"When we got to the target we would just press a button and the tanks would fall off the aircraft," the pilot explains. Ricci pushed the button as he dove his aircraft after the German.

"Either one or both [of the tanks] didn't fall off the aircraft," he says, "because when I turned sharply my plane went into a nose dive." Five thousand feet later he was able to recover from the dive. Another Me-109 had tracked him down and began blazing away with twenty millimeter cannon fire. The Mustang's tail assembly was hit and severely damaged. Ricci was in a nose dive again, unable to control his plane.

(Continued)

A drawing in tail gunner Sylvan Cohen's book shows one way to pass time—letter writing.

(COURTESY HARDY Z. BOGUE III)

"It was headed for the ground so I pulled off the canopy and tried to jump out—push myself out of the aircraft," he says, recounting those terrifying seconds. However, his parachute pack caught on something in the cockpit. He couldn't push himself out. The pilot estimated that the aircraft was hurtling five hundred or more miles an hour, straight towards the ground.

"I kept trying to get out, extricate myself," he explains. "And I couldn't, I couldn't, I couldn't! And finally I let go because I was exhausted. The moment I relaxed I just came out of the airplane. The wind just sucked me out of the airplane and I knew I must be very close to the ground."

His body hurtled through the air and instead of waiting for it to slow before opening the parachute, he immediately yanked on the ripcord. The opened chute swayed Ricci to the right once, then to the left once, and he was on the ground.

"I couldn't have been more than two hundred feet from the ground when I got out of the aircraft," he says, amazed. He was captured soon after landing in a field.

Behind the barbed wire of *Stalag Luft* I, Ricci traded his position as element leader for that of an art student in Colonel Greening's class.

Colonel Greening remained with the men between one and two hours each week as they sketched with small pencils.

"We would go and meet in the compound out in the yard," Ricci explains. "And Ross would be there and we would just go and follow him with pads and pencils to wherever he took us within the compound." Once a location had been selected by the art teacher, the men would begin their work. "We'd sketch away," Ricci says, "and he would give us a few directions, or talk about shadows, and we'd work away and he'd go around and watch everybody over their shoulder." Ricci was also recognized for his moral leadership and service to fellow prisoners. He too, received the "Flame of Freedom" medal from the Y.M.C.A.

Many of the budding artists found that their work with pencil on paper—whether in small tablets or full-size *Wartime Log* books—allowed them to mentally escape from their surroundings into the scene they were creating—at least for a short while.

The town of Barth as viewed from within the confines of *Stalag Luft* I by prisoner Al Ricci.
(COURTESY AL RICCI)

Pilot Ricci drew the small garden plot located at the end of one of the barracks at *Stalag Luft* I. Prisoners raised the vegetables, grown from seeds provided by the Red Cross, to supplement the prison diet. The tent was used to provide additional shelter for prisoners.

(COURTESY AL RICCI)

This guard tower at *Stalag Luft* I was a subject of study for pilot Al Ricci during an art lesson.

(COURTESY AL RICCI)

The interior of a barracks as drawn in Sylvan Cohen's *Wartime Log*.

Someday
Yuletide Bells
Will Ring
Again

Someday the Yuletide bells will ring again,
And once more there'll be laughter, joy and mirth,
Someday Christmas colors will sing again,
Those songs we love that tell of "Peace on Earth"
Someday hearts will be as they return again,
The husband father, son... the neighbors boy,
Someday Christmas lights will brightly burn again,
Illuminating faces filled with joy.

Prisoners drew their inspiration from many sources, including the *O.K.*, a German publication featuring prisoners' art and writing. Flight engineer Richard H. Stewart copied the cover art and a poem from the 24 December 1944 issue of *O.K.*

Sylvan Cohen's log, maintained at *Stalag* 17, features a comic pen and ink drawing of prisoners carrying a large bucket of soup as a turtle runs alongside in an effort to catch a drop.

(COURTESY HARDY Z. BOGUE III)

A pencil sketch in prisoner Richard H. Stewart's log book depicts the daily chore of getting water from the camp well. The prisoner with the bucket wears his German-issued dog tags suspended from his belt.

(COURTESY RICHARD H. STEWART)

WITH PERMISSION OF SOOY
MEYER

Drawings of women—both clothed and
unclothed—were often incorporated into
Wartime Log books. Airman Sylvan Cohen's
book contained a study of a "lady of the
night" at Piccadilly, as well as a drawing of a
young, skimpily clad woman with a fishing
pole. Navigator Edward Wodicka drew a
seated nude.

(COURTESY HARDY Z. BOGUE III, EDWARD WODICKA)

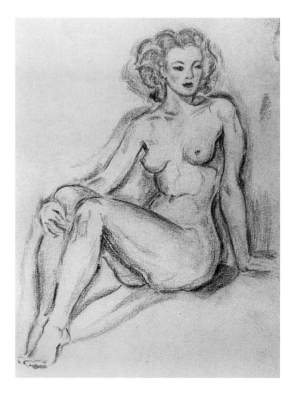

ESCAPE OF THE POET-ARTIST

Confronted with the daily boredom of *Stalag Luft* III prison life, Second Lieutenant Joseph Boyle turned to writing and drawing.

After being captured on 17 May 1943 following a bombing mission against submarine pens on the French coast, the B-17 copilot joined other American and British prisoners at the German prison camp located just south of Sagan, near the Polish border. The inactivity of the daily routine soon consumed him and he turned to writing poetry and drawing cartoons in the *Wartime Log* he acquired soon after his arrival in the camp.

The camp contained many talented British artists, and Boyle, a 1939 Lehigh University graduate who had contributed cartoons to his school's monthly *Lehigh Review*, became part of the art scene. His cartoons quickly gained popularity with fellow prisoners who requested that he draw some cartoons in their log books.

"They were momentarily impressed with some of the things that some of us did and they would want those things recorded in their log book," Boyle explains. The requests grew in number and the air officer often found a stack of log books waiting to be filled.

"When these things began to pile up in front of me until it was beginning to become a chore, I decided I'd better start getting paid some stipend for this," he said. "Or I'd simply be working full-time to amuse other people." A fraction of a chocolate D-bar was the usual remuneration for each cartoon drawn.

The subject matter of the cartoons came from everyday camp life. According to Boyle, clothing supplies were minimal so the prisoners had to improvise. Some of these outfits, Boyle recalls, were quite odd-looking. During his first winter in camp the prisoners were issued unusually colored and styled overcoats. They were robin egg blue, tight in the shoulders and flared at the bottom. The coats, which Boyle believes were manufactured for the French in World War I, became a subject for one of his cartoons.

Inspiration for his favorite humorous drawing came from an Independence Day prank. While the men were still asleep, three Americans staged a patriotic ride around the perimeter of the camp they shared with British prisoners.

Two of the trio dressed as a horse while the third, costumed as the American Revolutionary War patriot Paul Revere, sat on them, beating a metal spoon on a huge soup pan borrowed from the mess hall.

"The British are coming, the British are coming!" he exclaimed, over and over again. The commotion woke most of the camp and the celebration began. Many of the prisoners were looking forward to the American holiday as an excuse to celebrate, despite their imprisonment.

"They broke open these homemade brews that they'd been saving up for this occasion," Boyle says. The spirits were made from the raisins and prunes from Red Cross parcels, yeast obtained in trades with camp guards, and water.

"It was for special occasions that people would make these brews," the artist explains, "usually to celebrate Christmas or the anniversary of the day they got shot down. But in this case a lot of guys opened up the brews." The concoctions had a devastating effect on the prisoners, whose systems were unaccustomed to such potions.

"There was enough for an awful lot of them to get drunk and sick," Boyle recalls of the holiday. "There were bodies sprawled at various locations around the camp. It was a hot July day and they were sparsely clothed and lying around. It looked like some plague had struck the place in certain areas where there'd been more of an abundance of this kind of booze than in others." Boyle recorded the scene in a watercolor cartoon. (See page 91.)

Boyle also used humor in some of the poetry he wrote in his *Wartime Log* or contributed to the camp newspapers, the *Circuit* and *The Shaft*. The prisoner-produced publications were posted on the cook house wall so everyone could see them. Prisoners often copied poems and other items of interest from the paper into their log books.

"There were certain ideas that came to me

that I thought had a humorous angle and I would try and express it in a poem," Boyle explained of his work.

"And then there were more thought-provoking things that we did have plenty of time to think about. We saw a lot of our good friends get killed. It's a sad thing to deal with and poetry was in some ways a way to get some of those feelings off your chest." Out of Boyle's ten-man crew, only four survived.

When it came to writing poetry or drawing cartoons, time was on the side of the author or artist.

"There was a lot of time that you had to kill and some of us were better prepared to kill our time than others."

THANKS FOR THE MEMORY

Thanks for the memory
Of KLIM cans on parade
Of trinkets that we made
Of lack of cokes
Of corny jokes
And tunes the band has played
How lovely it was.

   Thanks for the memory
   Of a solitary cell
   Of evenings at appel
   Of washing clothes
   And Kriegie shows
   And bunks as hard as hell
   Oh thank you so much.

We kept mum at the interrogation
While we smoked cigarettes with a passion
Protecting the rights of our nation
But had enough at Dulag Luft

So thanks for the memory
Of a sing song Kriegie tune
Of General Ike in June
Of fighting Yanks
Of roaring tanks
I hope they get here soon
Oh! thank you so much.

We pull stumps 'til our backs are breaking
And we yell what a beating we're taking
But when we think of the dough we're making
Then the pain subsides—and our spirits rise

   So thanks for the memory
   of Stalag Number Three
   The home of you and me
   Where young souls burn
   And Kriegies yearn
   To once again be free
   Oh, thank you so much.

— FROM CLAUDIUS BELK'S *WARTIME LOG*
(COURTESY NORM FLAYDERMAN)

RUMOR MILL

With thousands of prisoners confined to a relatively small area, the prison camps holding American and other Allied flyers were rife with rumors. Many of the *Wartime Log* books kept by the captives featured cartoons depicting the spread of rumors. Usually the rumors added even more disappointment to the prisoner's life. Sometimes, however, they were the source of humor.

Robert McVicker, a B-17 ball turret gunner and owner of a *Wartime Log* book obtained in a high-card draw, was a prisoner in *Stalag Luft* 4, where the winter of 1944-1945 was quite severe. With several feet of snow on the ground and sub-zero temperatures, a rumor spread through the camp, sparking the curiosity of many of the prisoners. The Y.M.C.A., the rumor suggested, was about to deliver ice skates for the recreational use of the airmen.

McVicker and about fifty other men moved into action. They removed shutters from the barracks' windows and used them as snow shovels to clear and bank the snow. The prisoners got water from two nearby wells.

"We had a bucket brigade and we pumped those wells dry," explains McVicker. They poured water over the ground within the banked snow, where it quickly froze.

After several days of hard labor the project was completed and the ice rink glistened in the winter sunlight. While they waited for the skates, the bored prisoners prematurely took to the ice, falling and bruising themselves as they slipped on the slick surface in their shoes and boots.

Days passed and disappointment replaced the men's sense of anticipation.

"We never saw the skates," McVicker says wistfully. Such was the case with many of the rumors that circulated through the camps.

Gossip was exchanged at the camp latrine. Richard H. Stewart recorded the process of rumor spreading in this *Wartime Log* cartoon.

(COURTESY RICHARD H. STEWART)

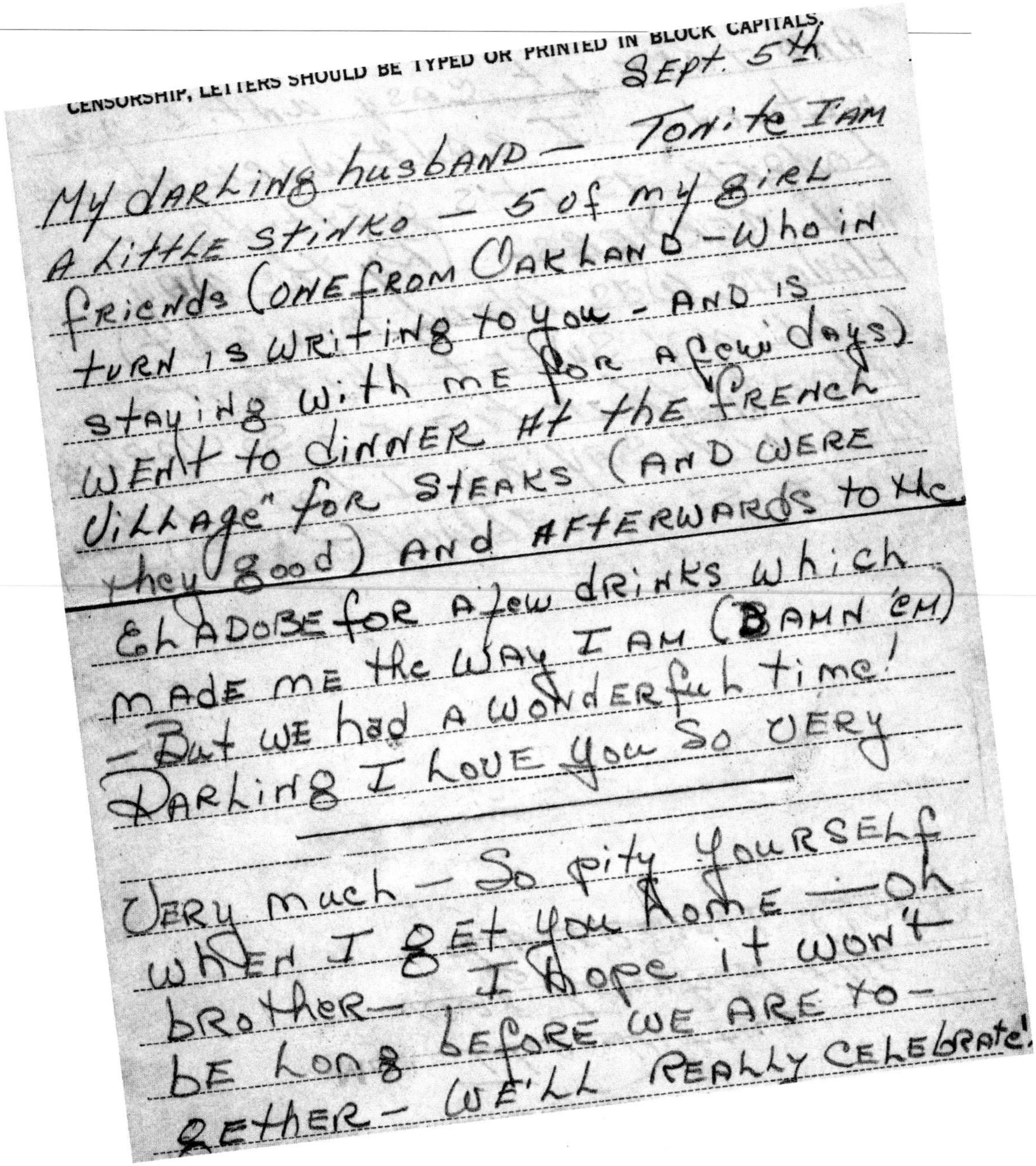

CENSORSHIP, LETTERS SHOULD BE TYPED OR PRINTED IN BLOCK CAPITALS.

Sept. 5th

My darling husband — Tonite I am
a little stinko — 5 of my girl
friends (one from Oakland — who in
turn is writing to you — and is
staying with me for a few days)
went to dinner at the French
Village" for steaks (and were
they good) and afterwards to the
El Adobe for a few drinks which
made me the way I am (Bamn 'em)
— But we had a wonderful time!
Darling I love you so very

very much — So pity yourself
when I get you home — oh
brother — I hope it won't
be long before we are to-
gether — we'll really celebrate!

Prisoners anxiously awaited news from
their families and often affixed letters
from home to the pages of their
Wartime Log books. One can only
imagine the reaction of the prisoner
who received this letter from his wife
about dining and drinking in a hometown restaurant.

(COURTESY BELTRONE COLLECTION)

HURTFUL HUMOR

Asense of humor was an important weapon in combatting the fear and boredom of a prisoner of war camp.

The *Wartime Log* books often contained excerpts gleaned from "Dear John" letters and other hurtful mail received by prisoners. Sometimes the items were posted in areas frequented by the men, such as latrines and mess halls. With time even the most painful messages became funny.

B-17 copilot Patrick Reams' *Wartime Log* included the following excerpts:

A P.O.W. received a sweater from a woman through the Red Cross and after writing her a letter of thanks, received the reply:
> "I am sorry to hear a prisoner of war received the sweater I knitted. I intended it for a fighting man."

From a lieutenant's father:
> "I knew I should have kept you at home and joined the Air Corps myself. Even when you were a kid I expected you'd end up in prison."

To an R.A.F. [Royal Air Force] sergeant from his fiancee:
> "You can consider our friendship at an end. I'd rather be engaged to a 1944 hero than a 1941 coward."

A relative to a prisoner:
> "I am enclosing a calendar. I thought it might come in handy as it has several years on it."

Lt. C.P.N. received the following from a girl he met in Florida two years ago and after one date hadn't seen or written to her.
> "I am going to spend the summer with your folks. They are fine and all your relatives are very kind. Your loving fiancee!"

From a lieutenant's wife:
> "I am as happy as can be without you!"

From flight engineer Richard H. Stewart's *Wartime Log*:

Letter from a P.O.W.'s fiancee:
> "Darling, I married your father. (signed) Mother."

Letter received by 1940 P.O.W. [British]:
> "Darling, I am glad you got shot down before flying got dangerous."

Letter from fiancee to P.O.W.:
> "Darling, I hope you are staying true to me."

Wife to British P.O.W. husband, a two-year captive:
> "Darling, I've just had a baby, but don't worry. The American officer is sending you cigarettes and he is bringing baby and I chocolate each day!"

Letter received from home:
> "You may be home sooner than we hoped!"

A prisoner's thoughts of home were always present. Richard Stewart drew this cartoon in his log book as a reminder of more pleasant times. (COURTESY RICHARD STEWART)

PASSING TIME

It was the bottom of the twenty-second inning and the score, well, nobody really cared. Another afternoon of "cow pasture" softball on the *Stalag Luft* 4 parade ground was about to end.

The game was described in that way by B-17 gunner Daniel Wilkerson, who was born and raised in the small, rural Virginia town of Mount Pleasant, located in the foothills of the Blue Ridge Mountains, near Roanoke. Prisoners played the game on the large, open area surrounded by barracks that was used in the morning and late afternoon for *appel*. The area became a field of dreams for the men who participated in the camp's recreational activities, another way of escaping from the tedious boredom of prison life.

Cow pasture ball was like the unstructured games played during childhood, games that went well beyond the regulation nine innings, games where the rules of play were often ignored.

"We played whenever we could . . . until everybody just got tired," Wilkerson recalls. There were no formal foul lines and scraps of wood served as bases. The War Prisoners Aid of the Y.M.C.A. provided balls and bats. It was the kind of game that almost everyone had played as a child.

"It was," as Wilkerson explains, "what we called back then 'cow pasture' ball. We improvised." In some American prison camps, softball was more structured and included umpires, organized leagues, and official team standings.

Besides softballs and bats, the Y.M.C.A. provided prisoners with a vast array of sports equipment. Volleyballs, soccer balls, ice skates, ice hockey sticks, golf clubs, and golf balls were just some of the other items provided.

The games were not without potential danger. When a ball was hit or thrown under the prisoners' barracks, permission to retrieve the ball had to be obtained from a guard. Otherwise, a player was likely to be fired upon.

"They were thinking you were trying to dig a tunnel or something," says Wilkerson, (who was shot down on 8 May 1944, on his eighteenth mission). "You had to be in sight at all times." Nevertheless, men often ignored the rule.

"We tried to watch to see where the guards were, sneak under, and get it out," the airman explains. Challenging camp regulations to retrieve a ball became a kind of contest within a contest.

The German captors seemed to enjoy these daily games even though they didn't play.

"They had as much fun watching as we did playing," Wilkerson said, "especially if somebody got hurt or something. They'd get a big kick out of a fight."

Walking around the compound proved to be one of the best forms of exercise for the prisoners. The walker's pace was often slow because the prisoners were malnourished and out of shape. Physical activity declined dramatically when food became scarce, especially when the Red Cross food parcels—designed to supplement the German rations that were provided—were not received regularly by the prisoners. Four men, and in some cases even more, had to share a parcel designed to feed one man for seven days. Wilkerson weighed almost 180 pounds when he entered the service, but only 135 pounds when liberated.

The prisoners constantly discussed the subject of food because they were hungry all the time.

"That caused you to have nightmares and dreams," Wilkerson explains. "Not only night dreams but daydreams." Upon entering the camp the aviator had received a *Wartime Log* book, one designed for use by British prisoners. Wilkerson

(Continued)

Athletic events and other games were an important part of prisoner life. Robert McVicker's *Wartime Log* illustrated the accomplishments of one of his camp's best athletes.

(COURTESY ROBERT MCVICKER)

BY WARREN

BARTER

6'3" ACE OF STALAG FOUR.

HE STOOD BY FAR AS THE OUT STANDING BASKETBALL PLAYER IN CAMP !!! A GREAT BALL-HANDLER AND PASSER

NO ONE COULD STOP HIM FROM CATCHING PASSES IN THE TOUCH FOOTBALL GAMES ☆ ☆ ☆

Hails From The Hoosier State

AT BASEBALL HE LOOKED GOOD ANY PLACE. ONE OF BEST HITTERS + PITCHER IN CAMP. !!!

LIVES NEAR MUNCIE, IND.

As Natural As A

DON'T BE SURPRISED TO SEE HIM IN THE MAJOR LEAGUES

devoted space in the book to record special recipes developed by prisoners to add more taste to their meals.

"After a while it got so that you had to be a little cautious about talking about good food because guys were getting on edge. They'd bust you if you mentioned something [about food]," explains McVicker. "Food was the biggest thing."

With nothing but time on their hands, the prisoners were desperate to pass the time between waking and going to sleep again. In addition to athletic equipment, the Y.M.C.A. also sent musical instruments into the prison camps. Airmen who had been professional musicians prior to the war formed musical groups to entertain the camp population. Theatrical supplies, also provided by the Y.M.C.A., were used in plays and musicals performed, and often written, by the prisoners.

Wilkerson, who had sung in high school, formed a quartet with three other prisoners. These were not formal productions, as some camp programs were, but rather impromptu events.

"We'd all get together for entertainment," he explains. Fellow prisoners gathered around to hear the quartet sing the popular songs of the day. They were the songs that had been popular before they were shot down or current tunes they had learned from recently captured airmen.

As with playing softball, the singing went on until the prisoners got tired.

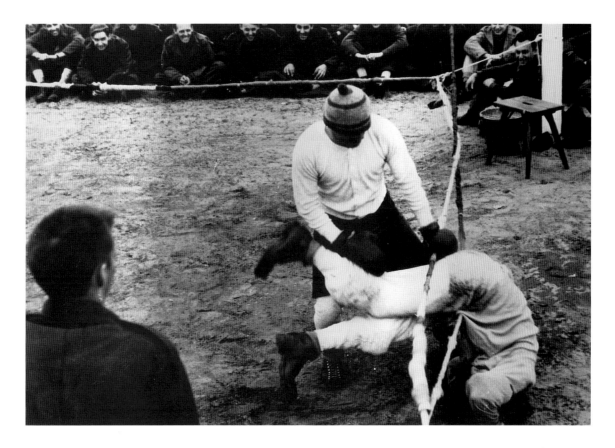

The Y.M.C.A. War Prisoners Aid organization provided a variety of sporting goods and equipment, including boxing gloves (above), to prisoners. The Y.M.C.A. also sent musical instruments for the entertainment of P.O.W.s (left). The photos on the opposite page show workers packaging the recreational equipment (top), and a theatrical production, supported by the Y.M.C.A., which also was a hit with the *Kriegies* (bottom).

(BOXING AND THEATER PHOTOS COURTESY DOROTHY FISHBURNE; OTHERS COURTESY YMCA OF THE USA ARCHIVES, UNIVERSITY OF MINNESOTA LIBRARIES)

LET'S MAKE A DEAL

While one prisoner offered another cigarettes for a pair of handcrafted lead pilot wings, another tried to convince a somewhat reluctant fellow officer to swap his A-2 leather flying jacket for more than a dozen chocolate D-bars. Both were lessons in prison camp economics.

Trading between prisoners was a way of life and also extended to the Germans charged with guarding the airmen. Second Lieutenant Patrick Reams found he was without a towel when he arrived at *Stalag Luft* I. The currency of exchange was cigarettes and D-bars, but Reams, a non-smoker just in from the German interrogation center, had neither. He did have a watch, an Elgin, which he traded for a towel and cigarettes, to be used in later trades.

Reams, who was shot down on 25 February 1944, a month after his twenty-eighth birthday, found the camp economy so fascinating that he devoted a full page of his *Wartime Log* book to a comparison of commodity values. The airman compared the value of certain commodities when he arrived with their value one year later in 1945.

Spam traded for sixty cigarettes in 1944, then ninety in 1945. English cocoa was marketed at forty cigarettes in 1944, compared to eighty in 1945 and Canadian jam, first offered for sixty cigarettes in 1944, had doubled in value to 120 by February 1945. The biggest jump concerned one of the favorite items in the Red Cross food parcels: the chocolate D-bar. One D-bar was worth fifty cigarettes in February 1944, but one year later had risen in value to four hundred cigarettes! The laws of supply and demand controlled the values. Food parcels were less frequently received during the last year of the war so prices rose. A continued influx of new prisoners further fueled the inflation.

Other items were also traded, and Reams noted that in February 1945, one pair of wings was worth two D-bars, a seventeen-jewel Elgin watch could be exchanged for twenty D-bars, and an A-2 jacket had a value of fourteen D-bars. For those who did not have the appropriate camp currency of chocolate or cigarettes, a five-dollar personal check, often written on a scrap of paper for collection at some future date, could purchase one bar of chocolate.

The *Wartime Log* was one of the most valued items in the camp, according to Reams. A number of books were allotted to his barracks but only one copy was apportioned to his room. He and his roommates drew cards to determine who would get the book. Reams drew the ace of spades: the book was his.

Sometime later another prisoner, one without a log book, approached Reams with an offer to trade ten cartons of cigarettes for the copilot's *Wartime Log*. Reams refused.

"It was a possession that I was determined to keep," he says of the coveted book.

Stalag Luft III artist Joseph Boyle drew a cartoon series of the camp's barter economy in October 1943. A prisoner is shown trading most of his clothing for a chocolate bar. Both parties seemed pleased with the end result.

(COURTESY JOSEPH BOYLE)

'THE WATCH'

Each compound was ringed by a series of guard towers. Germans armed with machine guns manned the structures, which often served as subjects for *Wartime Log* artists. This tower was drawn by an American prisoner in *Stalag Luft* III.

CONFOUND AND CONFUSE

The American aviator-prisoners possessed a wealth of talent. At *Stalag Luft* I it was not uncommon for those with an interest in comedy to entertain fellow prisoners whenever possible. One page in B-24 bombardier Jack Friend's log book was used to feature such a performance by a stand-up comedian. Another prisoner accompanied the comic on an accordion provided by the Y.M.C.A.

(COURTESY JACK FRIEND)

THE SHOW MUST GO ON

Theater was an important distraction at almost every German prison camp housing U.S. Army Air Force personnel. Those involved with producing the events spent numerous hours writing songs and jokes, building scenery out of discarded wooden Red Cross and Y.M.C.A. shipping crates, making or renting costumes, and rehearsing.

Other men devoted time to organizing seating and assigning tickets for each production. The shows, normally staged in the communal mess hall or chapel, could not accommodate the entire East compound of copilot Patrick Reams' *Stalag Luft* I at one performance. The prisoner population numbered in the hundreds and the theater was small.

Prisoners had to carefully plan the flow of theater-goers so that everyone in the compound could attend. Tickets had to be reserved ahead of time. Men sat on the wooden crates used to ship Red Cross food parcels. Tickets were printed in the nearby town of Barth and records were kept of the names of those men who received each admission. The men waited in long lines in front of the "barbed wire box office" to obtain their tickets.

Copilot Reams highlighted two *Stalag Luft* I musical comedies—*Hit the Bottle* and *So What*—in his *Wartime Log* book. Each production, with music performed by prisoners using donated Y.M.C.A. instruments, lasted about one-and-a-half hours and ran for several days. They were among many such plays in the camps.

Aviator Reams recalled that the *So What* production, staged by fellow-prisoner and B-24 bombardier John E. Friend, was a favorite among prisoners and German camp officials. (Lieutenant Friend had attended the University of Pennsylvania where he was chairman of the school's prestigious "Mask and Wig" theatrical society.)

The musical comedy was fast-paced and featured popular songs including the tune "Jenny," which made its debut in the Broadway production *Lady in the Dark*. Musicians heard songs on smuggled radio sets or over the compound's public address system. They transcribed the lyrics and musical scores for later performances. Prisoners who performed stand-up comic routines added their gag routines to the production.

A high-kicking cancan-style dance, known as "Tiller" dancing, was performed by prisoners dressed in German peasant girl costumes with colorful ruffled skirts. The costumes were rented from a Berlin costume house with funds earmarked for entertainment purposes.

The German camp commandant enjoyed these productions and was driven to the "theater" in a barouche carriage. He wore a very large and ornate amethyst ring on one hand and sat at front and center. Aviator Reams noticed the commandant taking picture after picture of the action, continuously returning to his camera bag for more film. After the performance the commandant asked the cast to pose for a group photo.

Men cheered, guffawed and whistled as high-stepping fellow prisoners, some purposefully mis-

(Continued)

cast by Lieutenant Friend because their size or shape added to the humor, energetically performed the dance routines. The men were receiving adequate Red Cross food supplies at that time and still had the physical strength for such antics.

At one point in the show the audience quieted as bombardier Friend, wearing a glittery silver dress, walked on the stage and began singing the seductive song, "Jenny." The very night before his final mission on 19 June 1944, the airman had seen Ginger Rogers perform the song in the movie version of *Lady in the Dark*.

The shows provided welcome relief from the monotony of camp life and allowed prisoners to briefly escape to more pleasant times. Lieutenant Friend pursued his interest in theater after the war and became a highly-regarded story and script editor for the Emmy-winning "Hallmark Hall of Fame" television productions.

(ARTWORK COURTESY JACK FRIEND, PATRICK REAMS)

BEHIND THE SCENES

B-24 pilot Robert Keller, who was imprisoned in the Center Compound of *Stalag Luft* III after being shot down on his fourth mission on 15 September 1943, sometimes used his theater work for covert activities.

The newsroom, where German army communiqués and maps drawn by prisoners were displayed on the walls, was located in the building that housed *Stalag Luft* III's theater. The newsroom was a valuable source of information for Germans and Americans alike.

Because his background was in construction, Keller was a natural choice for drawing maps and creating set designs. He also altered military uniforms, transforming them into costumes to be used in camp productions.

These duties offered Keller opportunities to help his fellow prisoners who were attempting escape. He used his position in the newsroom to draw detailed maps of escape routes.

"I was copying maps for the guys who were trying to escape. If the Germans came in on an inspection and saw me working on a map, and they'd say 'What the hell is that?' I'd say, 'It's for the newsroom. Go and look at them.' And they did."

The pilot used his position as costume maker to piece together civilian-looking garb for fellow prisoners who were attempting escape.

"We purposely did it in the theater so that if the Germans found any of it, we told them it was theater work. We said we were just working on the next show."

The *Stalag Luft* III Center Compound theater was used for more than theatrical productions and musical performances—maps and civilian clothing for escape attempts were created in a back room. Air officer Robert Keller (pictured in the above sketch by fellow prisoner John E. Zavisho) participated in the covert activities. The drawing's caption reads: "Workbench for theatrical design."

B-24 pilot Robert Keller reads a book in *Stalag Luft* III. This pencil sketch was drawn and given to the officer by fellow prisoner Les Breidenthal.

(COURTESY ROBERT KELLER)

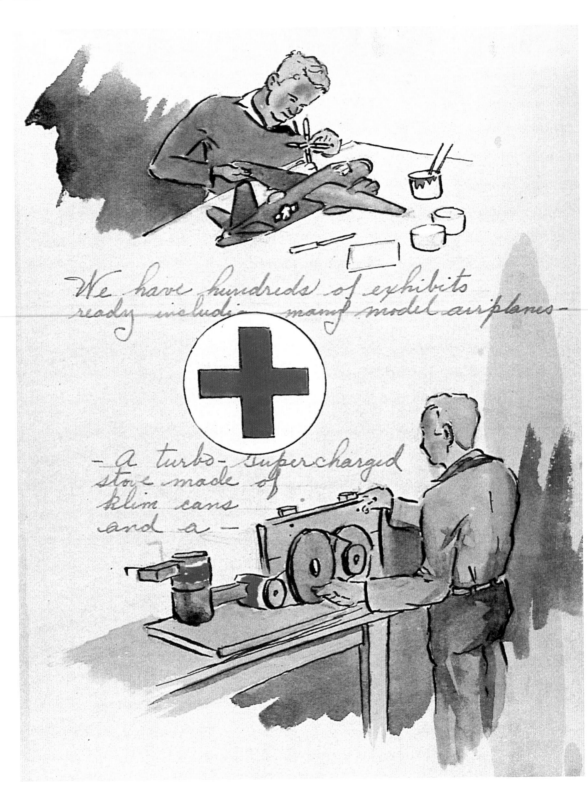

We have hundreds of exhibits
ready includi___ many model airplanes —

— a turbo-supercharged
stove made of
klim cans
and a —

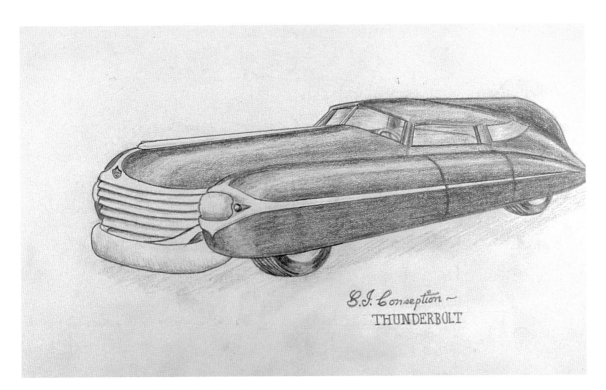

S.J. Conseption ~
THUNDERBOLT

Prisoners used pages of their log books to
speculate about homes and autos of the future.
A background in aviation often influenced the
car's styling. This vehicle, seemingly big and
strong, was named "Thunderbolt" in Richard
H. Stewart's *Wartime Log*. The *Thunderbolt* was
the rugged P-47 aircraft produced during the
war by the Republic Aviation Corporation of
Long Island, New York.

(COURTESY RICHARD H. STEWART)

Col. C. Ross Greening organized an exhibit of
prisoner-made crafts at *Stalag Luft* I and
thousands of men viewed hundreds of items
made in camp without tools. Model airplanes,
sculpture, insignia, paintings and drawings,
cartoons, and cooking utensils were displayed
for three days during the "Kriegie Kraft
Karnival" which took place 24–26 July 1944.
The colonel used a page of his *Wartime Log* to
record the exhibit preparations.

(COURTESY DOROTHY FISHBURNE)

The manufacture of insignia became a cottage industry in some camps. The insignia, mostly American and foreign aviators' wings, were made from lead removed from used corned beef containers. They were traded for tobacco products, chocolate D-bars, and other items. Display boards were sometimes used to mount collections of prisoner-made insignia. Flight engineer Richard H. Stewart traded another prisoner a wristwatch for this souvenir, a blue and white fabric-covered folder with nine wings. From top to bottom, left to right, the insignia are those of an American pilot, a British Pathfinder, a Royal Air Force pilot, a Czechoslovakian air gunner, a Soviet pilot, a Czechoslovakian pilot, a Polish pilot, an unofficial American prisoner of war badge, and a French pilot's device. The display board measures 9 1/2 inches wide and 8 inches high.

(COURTESY RICHARD H. STEWART)

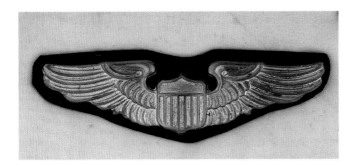

Some of the prisoner-made wings on Richard Stewart's display board feature gold highlights that may have come from the inside of toothpaste tubes. The thin metal was placed over a pair of wings to form a mold of the original. The wings shown here are (from top to bottom) those of an American pilot, a Royal Air Force pilot, a Czechoslovakian pilot, and an unofficial prisoner of war insignia.

(COURTESY RICHARD H. STEWART)

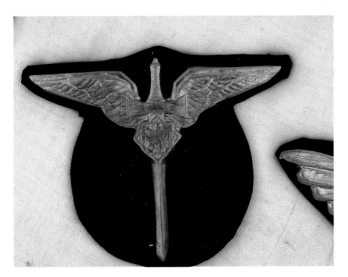

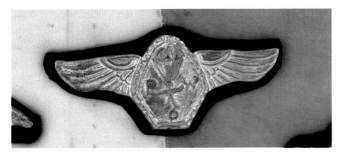

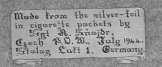

This triangular display board, measuring 8 inches wide and 11 inches high, includes 6 prisoner-made aviators' wings. From top to bottom, left to right, they are the wings of an American pilot, a Czechoslovakian pilot, a Czechoslovakian air gunner, a Royal Air Force pilot, a French pilot, and a Polish aviator. A small paper label affixed to the back of the board is neatly inscribed: "Made from the silver foil in cigarette packets by Sgt. A. Snajdr, Czech P.O.W., July 1944. Stalag Luft 1, Germany."

(COURTESY JOHN CONWAY)

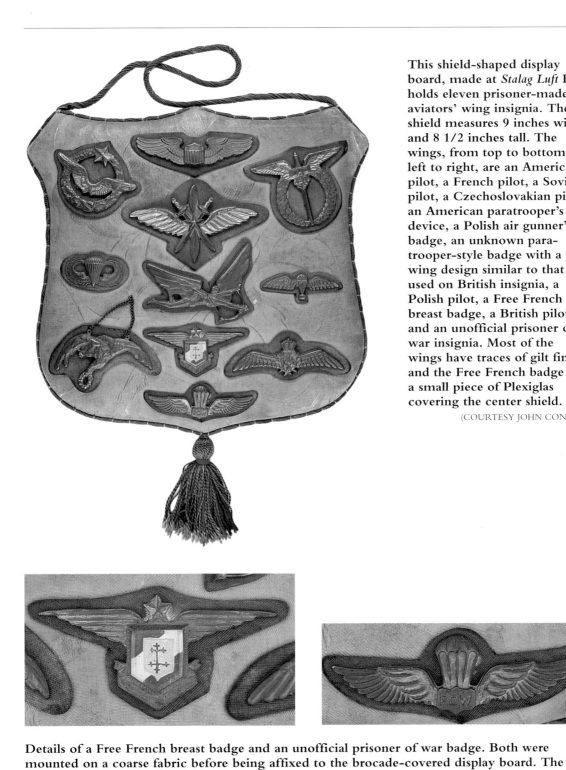

This shield-shaped display board, made at *Stalag Luft* I, holds eleven prisoner-made aviators' wing insignia. The shield measures 9 inches wide and 8 1/2 inches tall. The wings, from top to bottom, left to right, are an American pilot, a French pilot, a Soviet pilot, a Czechoslovakian pilot, an American paratrooper's device, a Polish air gunner's badge, an unknown paratrooper-style badge with a wing design similar to that used on British insignia, a Polish pilot, a Free French breast badge, a British pilot, and an unofficial prisoner of war insignia. Most of the wings have traces of gilt finish and the Free French badge has a small piece of Plexiglas covering the center shield.

(COURTESY JOHN CONWAY)

Details of a Free French breast badge and an unofficial prisoner of war badge. Both were mounted on a coarse fabric before being affixed to the brocade-covered display board. The reverse of the board was covered with a swatch of a gray-blue wool blanket. The piping and the decorative tassel were orange and blue.

(COURTESY JOHN CONWAY)

A *Stalag Luft* III prisoner remembers a Niagara Falls honeymoon. This sentimental watercolor by prisoner James R. Regan was given to B-24 pilot Robert Keller.

JUST DREAMING

Sometimes I get to dreaming
  When there's not much else to do;
And just as sure as night meets day,
  I always dream of you.

I dream of all the things we said
  The things we planned to do;
I remember all the things we did,
  The freedom that we knew.

I like to dream of happy days
  That belong to just we two;
It kinda gives these dreary hours,
  A little brighter hue.

Perhaps it's not too much to dream
  That I'll come home to you;
And if I do I'll know for sure,
  That sometimes dreams come true.

— FROM CHARLES WILLIAMS'S *WARTIME LOG*

The loneliness of P.O.W. life was captured by Colonel Greening in this self-portrait. He has just received a letter and daydreams about the prospects of being reunited with his wife.

Following the Allied invasion of Europe on 6 June 1944, rumors about liberation spread throughout P.O.W. camp populations. Prisoner Claudius Belk used a page in his log book to record how rumor soon became fact, all within a matter of minutes.

(COURTESY NORM FLAYDERMAN)

A prisoner looks hopefully toward the landscape beyond the bounds of the camp and its barbed wire fences. This was the last drawing B-17 gunner Sylvan Cohen commissioned for his *Wartime Log*. The aviator told his stepson Hardy Z. Bogue III that the higher ground on the horizon reminded him of neutral Switzerland.

(COURTESY HARDY Z. BOGUE III)

Holidays were especially lonely and discouraging. B-24 bombardier Jack Friend, a prisoner in *Stalag Luft* I, created this moving watercolor of how it felt to be in his camp during the 1944 Christmas season. The barbed wire fence is outside his barracks' window, lights illuminate the chapel in the background, and a clear sky is filled with bright stars to convey the hope of tomorrow.

THE NIGHT BEFORE CHRISTMAS

'Twas the night before Christmas
And down in the block
Some dreary old Kriegie
Sat darning a sock.

> *No need to place it*
> *By the chimney with care*
> *No hope that St. Nicholas*
> *Would ever be there.*

None of the merriment
Was left undone
To hide their feelings
All joined in the fun.

> *Carols of Christmas tide*
> *Sung loudly by all*
> *Made the whole building shudder*
> *From corner to hall.*

Snacks in the making
For a midnight delight
And the boys celebrating
Far into the night.

> *Tomorrow was Christmas*
> *As every man knew*
> *And each was determined*
> *He wouldn't be blue.*

So thus it continued
'Midst dull yellow light
A merry Christmas to all
At least for tonight.

— FROM CLAUDIUS BELK'S *WARTIME LOG*
(COURTESY NORM FLAYDERMAN)

WAR OF WITS

Three American air officers stood on the parade ground in the *Stalag Luft* I prison camp and eyed the Luftwaffe guards in the tower. The battle of wits was about to begin.

The American P.O.W.s began their act of passive resistance by cutting the ends from an empty food can in order to form a tube. Next, they fashioned a tripod from scrap wood and positioned the can on top of it so that it resembled a surveyor's quadrant. They tied a piece of string around a rock and placed a piece of paper on another scrap of wood to make it look like a clipboard.

Props in hand, the trio positioned themselves between the barracks and the barbed wire fence. In full view of the German guard towers, they began their "survey" of the compound.

"One guy took the piece of paper and board and stood next to the guy with the tripod," prisoner Roy Wendell, who was one of the "surveyors" explains. "The third one went near the barbed wire with the rock on a string." Fellow prisoners looked quizzically at the three.

"We yelled to each other, 'to the left, to the left. More. More. Okay, right there.' And then he would say, Thirty-two, and the other guy would write down thirty-two, and then you would move to another spot so that you were ostensibly surveying." The guards noticed the antics. Were these prisoners planning another tunnel?

"The guards were up in the tower," Wendell recalls. "There would be one up there, then two, then three, and they all were talking to each other, looking at us, and we'd keep on doing this, this farce. Moving around, calling numbers, and counting. And the Germans didn't know what to do about it." Finally, the guards moved into action.

"They sent a squad in, and they came up to us and they confiscated our can, the rock with the string, and the piece of paper. They didn't say anything, they just impounded our rock on the string and everything else. It was fun for us and it kept a whole gaggle of Germans busy."

The three aviators had participated in a form of provocation known as goon-baiting. The prisoners called German officers and soldiers in the camp "goons;" guard towers were known as goon boxes. When the Germans asked what the term goon meant, they were told it was an abbreviation—G.O.O.N.—for German officer or noncom.

Wendell's and his comrades' antics cheered up other prisoners according to psychologist and former P.O.W. Dr. Charles Stenger.

He explains that goon-baiting was undertaken "to show anger and to feel that you had some power and that you weren't helpless." But, prisoners had to be careful not to take goon-baiting too far.

"The problem was to do what would make you feel adequate and make the German guards or others frustrated, without pushing it to the point that you might be badly beaten or injured," explains Stenger. "In a sense, people in prison camps test the limits."

The digging of escape tunnels and other devious activities gave prisoners a sense of control and power. Few airmen ever successfully left the camp by escaping through a tunnel, but German guards were certainly frustrated by the attempts, no matter how futile. German prison officials failed to understand the sense of accomplishment American prisoners earned from goon-baiting.

The Germans had been taught by the state and the church to fear and obey authority. The German military was steeped in tradition, and those entering the service were reminded that "the soldier doesn't think, the soldier obeys!"

(Continued)

Reveille at *Stalag* 17 is shown in Sylvan Cohen's log book. During the subsequent *appel* (or roll call) prisoners sometimes practiced passive resistance by disrupting the head count.

(COURTESY HARDY Z. BOGUE III)

The American soldier, on the other hand, had not experienced the same fear of government authority. Having grown up in a society founded on individual freedoms, he placed more importance on his personal thoughts and beliefs. He was in the service because he believed freedom and democracy—the very principles that enabled him to be independent—were being challenged. The American soldier's ingenuity and strong sense of self kept him from "going around the bend," a phrase used to describe a captive who had lost his senses. The prisoner used his mind to confound and confuse the enemy, and, in the process, kept himself sane.

Most barracks buildings were constructed several feet off the ground to keep prisoners from constructing tunnels under them. At night the guards, sometimes accompanied by dogs, crawled under the structures in an attempt to overhear conversations that betrayed important information concerning the war effort. When the airmen learned of the eavesdropping, they took action.

They poured hot water through the cracks in the barracks' wooden floor in order to scald the guards and their dogs. If a scrap of food could be sacrificed the prisoners laced it with pepper and threw it under the barracks. A dog would find the morsel, smell it, and be overcome with sneezing, causing the animal's head to strike the underside of the building's floor—to the delight of the prisoners.

Germans often used the crawl space of the barracks' attic to eavesdrop. To counter this form of intelligence-gathering, which was usually conducted at night, prisoners threw broken glass and used razor blades into the area crawl space. They knew at once when somebody was snooping above them because they could hear painful cries as the sharp objects cut into the intruder's flesh.

American copilot Patrick Reams recalled an incident in his camp following the arrival of a new senior officer. The new man was taken to the man he was replacing and while they were talking, one of the bolts holding the barracks wall together fell into the room. A junior officer reinserted the bolt into the wall, but it promptly fell out again. The Americans realized an informant, known as a "ferret," was listening in on the conversation.

With a pair of tongs, the out-going senior officer picked the bolt up off the floor and placed it in the stove. When sufficiently heated, the bolt was reinserted into the wall.

"The next thing we knew, there was a loud yell because the German had tried to shove it back out again with a finger and burned [himself]," Reams says. "A rifle shot came through the room and that was that."

Reams had another encounter with a German rifle while in *Stalag Luft* I, one that led to the disappearance of an unpopular camp guard. One morning when the signal was given for the men to fall out of their barracks and assemble on the camp's parade ground for roll call, the guard positioned himself, as was his custom, along the end of the barracks so he could encourage the Americans to vacate the building faster.

The guard stood with his rifle slung over his shoulder, muzzle pointed upward. During the commotion of the call to *appel*, Reams reached out the open window and carefully dropped dirt and several tiny pebbles mixed with a few drops of water into the bore of the weapon's barrel. The guard was so preoccupied with the prisoners' exodus from the building, that he was unaware of the copilot's antics.

In the following days the guard was nowhere to be seen. When prisoners asked other guards about his absence, they were told that the barrel of the man's weapon had blown apart during firing practice.

"I figured they didn't clean their gun every day," Reams explains. "By the time he went out there, after two weeks in the hot sun, the stuff had all baked hard in the barrel and the gun just exploded."

Roll call seemed a natural time for such pranks to take place. When the head count was being taken by guards, prisoners stooped down to tie a shoelace, throwing off the count. When the recount was taken, they would all stand again so that the two counts were different. Bombardier Charles Williams says that prisoners often dug small holes in the parade ground and covered

When snow fell and temperatures dropped, thoughts turned to winter games. The Y.M.C.A. War Prisoners Aid organization provided ice skates and hockey sticks to some camps. The broken window at far right—patched with cloth—may have been caused by an errant puck. The Germans sometimes tried to bill prisoners for such damage.

(COURTESY AMERICAN RED CROSS)

them with sticks and leaves so they couldn't be seen. When the German responsible for counting the formation walked by, he would often step into these traps and stumble.

Gunner Dan Wilkerson remembers men dropping scraps of paper encoded with bits of sentences meant to be understood as escape plans. If ferrets or goons found these scraps of paper, prison officials made another head count. Although it was an inconvenience for the prisoners, it was an even bigger problem for their captors.

Copilot Joseph Boyle was present during one winter roll call when the camp commandant, accompanied by a member of the Gestapo, entered the snow-filled parade ground in a horse-

drawn sleigh at *Stalag Luft* III. The sleigh was magnificent, according to Boyle. It was heavily upholstered with fine leather. The solidly built horse was immaculate. The camp commandant and the Gestapo officer left the sleigh after the head count had been taken and a group of prisoners gathered around the vehicle for a closer inspection. Fifteen minutes later all the prisoners were called out to the parade ground again, where they were told by the senior officer that a serious infraction had occurred.

"It turned out that this commandant had a Luger pistol and a pair of gauntlets in the sleigh and they were missing," Boyle said. "Our CO [commanding officer] said that it would be a very,

very serious situation if these items weren't some- how found quickly." The number of guards around the camp's perimeter had been doubled and many of them carried machine guns. Before being dismissed the men were told they had ten minutes to find the items. When ten minutes had elapsed the men returned to the parade ground. The sleigh was inspected and the pistol and gauntlets were found in their proper places.

The Germans used solitary confinement to punish prisoners for committing infractions of camp regulations. So many infractions were recorded, however, that a prisoner often had to wait up to six months or more before he could serve his time in the cooler, a special room where solitary confinement was served. There were that many men on the solitary confinement waiting list.

American prisoners kept themselves occupied in a variety of ways while they waited. Attending religious services was an important part of their lives. They had lived through the harrowing experience of being shot out of the sky, they had watched fellow crewmen perish, yet they, for some reason, had survived. They were thankful for their own survival and their gratitude renewed their interest in religion.

Prisoners also had housekeeping duties such as cleaning and cooking. They might also be engaged in digging a tunnel, spreading dirt, or distracting the guards by starting arguments. They would work in *Wartime Log* books or participate in any number of classes taught by fellow prison- ers.

The Y.M.C.A., other welfare organizations, and the P.O.W.s' families sent books that were placed in a communal room that served as a camp library. Some of the men listed the titles of the books they borrowed from the library in their *Wartime Log* books. One prisoner listed almost three hundred volumes.

Prisoners also put on plays using scripts bor- rowed from the library or scripts they had written themselves. They designed and constructed scenery and sets—often out of wooden Red Cross shipping boxes. The productions were scheduled so that all members of the camp com-

pound could attend. Musical productions utilized the talents of the camp's musicians and were espe- cially popular.

The athletic equipment provided by the Y.M.C.A. also enabled the prisoners to pass many otherwise boring hours and to stay fit. The Y.M.C.A. even created a sports medal that was awarded to men in camp for significant athletic achievements.

American resourcefulness was never more evi- dent than in athletics. When clip-on ice skates arrived in one *Stalag Luft* I compound, no formal ice rink existed. Yankee ingenuity prevailed when prisoners created one by banking snow and carry- ing water to the area from a nearby fire pool. But the skating came to an abrupt end after guards found that a fence had been cut with wire cutters made from ice skate blades. The Germans imme- diately confiscated all ice skates.

A Y.M.C.A. shipment of golf clubs and a few golf balls arrived in *Stalag Luft* III one day. According to prisoner Joseph Boyle, a number of the men eagerly took the clubs and balls, formed driving tees by mounding dirt, and then proceed- ed to drive the balls over the main fence and out of the camp.

"So that was the end of golf," Boyle laughs. "The golf season started and stopped all within the first fifteen minutes."

Boyle's roommate, who had played golf before the war, devised a way to make more golf balls. He and Boyle cut a piece of rubber from the heel of a discarded boot and wrapped it with the cot- ton twine from the inside of a torn softball. They made the outer shell of the ball from the top of a worn-out boot or from an old basketball. They formed the shell into a figure eight shape that had been drawn to scale on a piece of homemade graph paper. A small nail was used to poke holes in the covering and linen thread and a curved needle, obtained from a prisoner who fixed shoes in camp, were used to sew it all together.

"We sewed up these covers and pushed the ball inside and finished sewing it up," Boyle explains. "Then we'd roll the ball on a table top under a book, and dampen it, and roll it, until it finally shrunk tight. We had a golf ball that we

Russian prisoners cleaned the latrines with a large, heat-powered vacuum tank. The by-product of the process forced prisoners to run for cover.

(COURTESY ROBERT MCVICKER)

could hit fifty or sixty yards with some consistency with an eight iron."

The golfers buried an empty food can in the ground between the barracks, smoothed the dirt around it and moved about fifty yards away. They competed to see who could hit a hole in one and if someone was successful, he was awarded a prize, usually a square or two of a Canadian chocolate bar.

"The golf balls that we made provided us with a considerable amount of recreational entertainment for a month or so," Boyle recalls. The game ended when the club turned up missing one day. "I think somebody stole the eight iron. This was not the kind of thing that was possible to divide equally among two thousand men."

Creativity and resourcefulness made the uncertainty of living more bearable. Optimism also helped.

Navigator Roy Wendell was twenty years old when he took pen in hand in his sparsely furnished *Stalag Luft* I barracks on 5 March 1945. Red Cross food parcels were seldom distributed despite the existence of thousands of unissued packages in a nearby warehouse, and rumors, some none too encouraging, circulated concerning the prisoners' fate. Word was passed that the men were to be shot as a reprisal for the devastating mid-February Allied bombing raid on Dresden. Prisoners and camp guards both became

anxious. As the days passed each group became more and more concerned about its safety.

Despite these conditions, Wendell neatly printed a letter—addressed to the Notre Dame admissions office—on one of the three prisoner of war letter forms he was entitled to use each month. (The original correspondence is preserved in Notre Dame's archives.)

"Although I am at present a prisoner of war in Germany," he wrote, "I would like to avail myself of this opportunity to submit my name for enrollment in the Engineering College of Notre Dame, with the idea in mind that I will be able to be discharged from the Army upon the conclusion of the war in Europe." The air officer asked that a response from the school be forwarded to his parents in Woodhaven, New York.

Almost one year later the school received Wendell's request, and on 25 February 1946, long after the war had ended, the admissions director sent a letter to the aviator's parents.

"If your son has returned safely I offer you my congratulations and if he is still interested in pursuing his studies at Notre Dame I suggest that he write me immediately and I shall do what I can to further his ambition," the official wrote.

Wendell did so and graduated in 1950, not with a degree in engineering, but with one in journalism. His optimism as a prisoner had been rewarded.

LEAD WINGS AND TIN PLATES

Behind barbed wire with lots of time on their hands, the Army Air Force prisoners manufactured many basic living necessities as well as camp souvenirs.

They made eating and cooking utensils, which were scarce in the camps. If plates were not available, the tin cans from Red Cross food parcels were substituted. Prisoners took them apart carefully and hammered them into plates, bowls, and cups. Eating utensils, including knives, forks, and spoons, were also fashioned from tin food cans. The challenge posed by materiel shortages was welcomed by the prisoners.

"That was appealing to most of us when we found there were ways to do certain things or make certain things that we lacked," explains co-pilot Joseph Boyle, former *Stalag Luft* III prisoner.

Food was heated more quickly and efficiently with small stoves that used a forced air system devised by prisoners. The stoves were fashioned from discarded Red Cross food cans.

First Lieutenant Elmer T. Lian, a B-17 pilot who was shot down 27 September 1944 while flying a mission over Mannheim, Germany, spent the rest of the war in *Stalag Luft* I. He became quite familiar with the ingenuity displayed by fellow prisoners, especially those who made wing insignia. According to Lian, wings and other insignia were produced primarily as camp souvenirs. Some prisoners replaced their wings with the camp insignia since theirs had been lost.

Enterprising prisoners often worked in pairs collecting discarded Red Cross food cans. The cans were either seamed with a bead of lead or had a drop of lead covering a small hole at the top. Corned beef cans usually had this second type of seal.

"They would take a table knife, which was made of steel, and then they'd sharpen it and just scrape the lead out of the crevice," Lian remembers. "Then they'd break open the seam and they'd scrape more lead out so they got all the lead." Applying heat to loosen the drop of lead on the top of the can was another technique used to salvage the material from that portion of the can.

The process took time, but that wasn't a problem for prisoners of war.

"Every time you were doing something you took an interest in it," Lian explains. "I think it made a person feel good."

Prisoners created a mold for whatever wing or insignia they were making. The mold was made from a combination of fine sand and a material similar to clay, according to Lian. An original pair of wings or other insignia was pressed into the mixture to create a detailed impression mold.

Small stoves, also made from discarded Red Cross food tins, were used to melt the lead. The forced air blowers created the intense heat needed to burn the small, compressed coal dust briquettes which were sparingly provided by the Germans, primarily for the use of heating food. Once molten, the lead was poured into the mold and the insignia was formed.

"If something didn't turn out just right in this process," the pilot explains, "there was no big problem. All they would do was do it over again. They had plenty of time."

After the molten lead was poured into the mold, the prisoner leveled off the exposed back of the insignia, and while still soft, inserted small metal posts or a safety pin into the surface. Small holes had to be made in the posts so that a pin could be inserted through them to hold the wings on the uniform. The safety pin was easier to use, but was liable to break away from the wings' body. Lian estimates that it took the lead from ten cans to make one insignia.

The sand and clay molds were used in the production of standard wings. Other insignia, such as the pilot's wings with "POW" and "*Stalag Luft* I" in the center shield, or the wings with the parachute above the center shield, had to be made using a wooden carving of the design.

"They'd carve the whole thing out and make it look just like a real pair of wings," Lian said.

Prisoners also made original insignia—insignia not produced by the commercial firms. These examples of unofficial decorations both have the letters "POW"—for prisoner of war—in the center shield. Simulated barbed wire strands were also used in some designs. Both insignia measure 3 inches wide.

(BELTRONE COLLECTION)

According to Second Lieutenant Reams, who was also imprisoned at *Stalag Luft* I, there was a third method for making the insignia.

The gold lining of empty toothpaste tubes was placed over a pair of wings or other insignia and a pointed object, such as a sharpened twig, was used to press the malleable toothpaste tube material into the original insignia to form a hollow duplicate of the wings with a gold-colored finish. One postwar American Y.M.C.A. publication, *The Yankee Kriegies,* also reported that wings were made with the lead foil from packages of cigarettes. This foil was also melted and poured into molds.

Prisoners often traded wings and other insignia for chocolate D-bars or cigarettes. One D-bar usually bought one pair of wings, according to pilot Lian.

"The guy who made the wings, you'd give him a D-bar, and he'd give you the wings," he says, explaining the camp's barter system. "Then he'd take the D-bar and he could buy something else. In fact, he might even trade it to the Germans for something." Sometimes an egg or two, a cigarette lighter, or a bit of kerosene could be obtained from a German.

As bombing of the German transportation system increased during 1944, the flow of Red Cross food parcels to the camps began to slow. Fewer parcels getting into the camps meant a smaller amount of available lead. The manufacture of wings drew to a close.

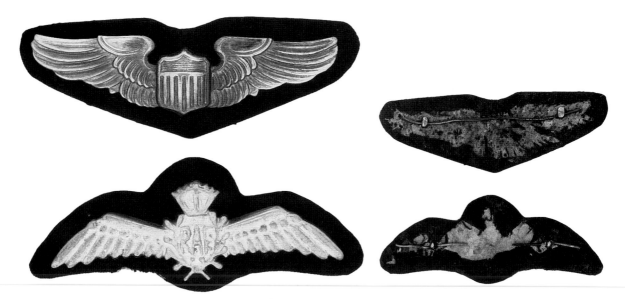

These photos show examples of prisoner–made, lead insignia. In the upper left is an American pilot's wing measuring 3 inches wide. Beneath is a British pilot's wing, measuring 2 7/8 inches wide. The backs of the insignia are shown at right.

(COURTESY BELTRONE COLLECTION)

These photos compare a bombardier's wing insignia made at *Stalag Luft* I (top) with a sterling silver wing insignia manufactured by a commercial insignia firm in the United States. The reverse sides show the differences in finish details and attachment devices.

(POW WING COURTESY RON BURKEY, JR; COMMERCIAL WING COURTESY BELTRONE COLLECTION)

Another variation of insignia design featured the name of a prison camp and a parachute. These wings were crafted at *Stalag Luft* I. The wing with the parachute measures 2 7/8 inches wide, the other is 3 inches wide.

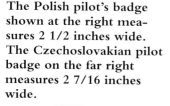

The Polish pilot's badge shown at the right measures 2 1/2 inches wide. The Czechoslovakian pilot badge on the far right measures 2 7/16 inches wide.

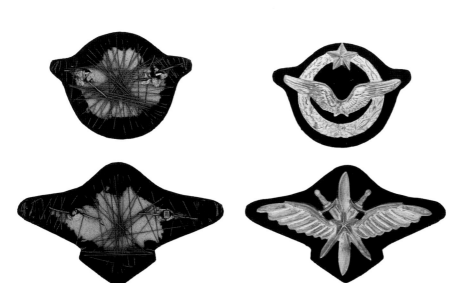

A French pilot's badge (top) and a Soviet pilot's badge (bottom) were also made of lead collected from food cans. The French insignia measures 3 3/8 inches wide and the Soviet insignia is 2 1/4 inches wide.

THE SOUND OF MUSIC

Claire Cline, a twenty-six-year-old B-24 pilot imprisoned in *Stalag Luft* I, created what is perhaps the most well-known souvenir to have come out of the German prison camps.

Cline, who was shot down and captured on 22 February 1944, spent three months making his souvenir, a violin that was later played by some of the most noted violin virtuosos in the United States.

Cline, who had some experience making violins, needed material and tools to accomplish the project. He gathered wood for the violin from a number of sources in the prison camp, including the three-quarter-inch-thick slats that supported the straw-filled mattress of his bunk. He carved these into the shape of the outer portion of the violin. He made the instrument's neck from a confiscated table leg. Klein obtained glue by scraping dried mucilage from crude cabinets and furniture provided for the prisoners' use by the Germans. He added drops of water to the scrapings and heated the mixture to form a usable adhesive.

"That was our lament over there," he explains. "We didn't have tools to work with." So he took stock of other available implements and improvised. He made a wood chisel by grinding a table knife and sharpened it with a rock. He used pieces of broken glass as scrapers. And in the dead of night, when men slept in their bunks, the pilot became a trader, exchanging cigarettes with camp guards for other tools, including a good pocket knife for finer scraping and sand paper for the finishing touches.

"It was a rather slow process," he says of the project. "An extremely slow process." He estimates that it took him between three and four months to make the instrument. Most of the time he worked in his barracks, but sometimes, when the weather was pleasant, he sat outside patiently working on his project. His progress continued to amaze fellow prisoners.

He traded more cigarettes for sheep gut strings and a bow to play the instrument, because, as the pilot explains, "there was no way to make those."

Once it was completed, the violin's music filled the pilot's barracks. Later, during a national tour of a prisoner of war crafts exhibit, professional musicians played Cline's violin for thousands of spectators. The instrument became the highlight of the tour and was applauded for its superior tonal quality.

As for Cline, he simply looked at his unusual achievement as a way to pass the time behind barbed wire. "It was just something for my own amazement," he says modestly of the accomplishment.

Prisoner of war Claire Cline poses with the violin he made while imprisoned at *Stalag Luft* I. A small penknife he used to make the instrument rests on his right leg.

WILLIE GREEN AND HIS FLYING MACHINE

This is the fable of Willie Green
Who invented a Kriegie flying machine.
'Tis as weird a tale as ever you heard
Yet I'll swear by the truth of every word.

The man who first heard it, suspicious as I,
Swore by his chocolate 'twas all a great lie.
But imagine his surprise, the gleam in his eyes,
When Willie's machine was seen to fly.

The parts were gathered—tis no secret now—
But Willie alone knows the secret how.
They were hidden away in corners and places
While he carved away on the spars and braces.

The tin can piles were low indeed
When W.G. performed his deed.
There still is talk of that famous day
As the last KLIM-tin was hidden away.

The engine was the first of the plane to be made
With crankshaft of steel from the missing spade.
While in KLIM-can cylinders with mighty sound
The butter can pistons went up and down.

The flashy propeller so aerodynamic
Was carved from a board in the barracks attic.
While the peculiar strand that made the ignition
Was a length of barbed-wire from the compound
partition.

Fuel was no problem to a man with a head
And Willie got gas from cabbage and bread.
In case of emergency, Willie held,
The thing could easily be Rocket-propelled.

The side of the bed the fuselage made
The stick, the handle of the fore-mentioned spade.
The instruments, it could be seen at a glance
Was none other than the seat of Willie's pants.

Two locker doors the wings did make
With dihedral taper and negative rake.
And a Red Cross box from a racket source
Served as the tail for his flying horse.

The question of wheels was mighty hot
Till Willie remembered the communal pot.
While Kriegies were wondering how it disappeared
Willie's machine became tricycle geared.

There were no guns on Willie's steed
Its only defense was its excessive speed.
To weigh down the tail our hero used
A size "12" pair of British shoes.

And when it was done our Willie cried
"Enough, enough, I'm satisfied."
And one dark night when conditions were best
Willie's machine was put to the test.

The prop turned over, the engine caught
"Aha," said Willie, "twas not for naught."
The plane jumped forward, started to fly
And was over the fence in the wink of an eye.

The guard yelled "Verboten" and started to shoot
But all his efforts were as good as "Kapoot."
Willie flew on and into the dark
Toward Ellis Island and Battery Park.

The plane flew on until Willie spied
The lights that marked the other side.
He felt so good and oh so free
His Red Cross box fell into the sea.

A crowd was there when he landed his crate
"Where am I?" he asked. "It sure looks great."
"Why where," they cried, "were you headed for?"
"This my boy—is Stalag Luft IV."

— BY EMMETT DEDMON, FROM EDWARD WODICKA'S *WARTIME LOG*
(COURTESY EDWARD WODICKA)

This caricature of a B–17 was drawn in Patrick Reams's *Wartime Log*.
(COURTESY PATRICK REAMS)

The Germans moved *Stalag Luft* 4 prisoners to *Stalag* 7A, Moosburg, where, on 29 April 1945, they were liberated after a short but deadly fight between American tank units and defenders of the German town. A group of relieved former prisoners relaxes in front of one of the camp's empty guard towers.

"CAN IT BE OVER..."

Allied aircraft attract the attention of *Stalag* 17 prisoners in this sketch from Sylvan Cohen's *Wartime Log*. The airmen may be on their way to the air raid trenches within the compound.

JOURNEY TO LIBERATION

Liberation for the majority of U.S. Army Air Force prisoners of war occurred between 29 April and 3 May 1945.

Noncommissioned officer P.O.W.s from *Stalag* 17B began the march from their camp near Krems, Austria, to a Russian prison camp at Braunau, Austria, on 8 April. On 3 May the camp was liberated by advancing American forces.

Prisoners in *Stalag Luft* I at Barth, Germany, made contact with advancing Russian troops on 1 May after the German guards pulled out of the camp late in the evening of 30 April.

B-24 bombardier Jack Friend recorded the excitement of the events leading up to the *Stalag Luft* I liberation in his *Wartime Log*. He wrote on one of the unnumbered, heavy stock pages in the book's center section:

"I write this hurriedly and without concentration—only as a thing, a time to remember. I do not know what sort of exhilaration takes me, if it is mere excitement or apprehension—the Germans are leaving—the Russians are coming. We have been told we can expect them at any moment, tonight or tomorrow. The Germans have been excited all day and hordes of refugees are leaving in long lines of disordered confusion. They are blowing up the radio equipment in the flak school and gutting the entire building. The explosions have blown in some of the windows and many men are digging trenches just in case.

"Can it be over—this is in my mind all engrossing and omnipresent. The sky is full of German planes and yet there is no sign of the Russians except the panicked fleeing of the Germans. The swarms of our boys run from place to place with rumors—each explosion brings wide-eyed men flying from the room crowding to see what is going on. The radio has gone off—the water is expected to at any moment—what's more the guards from the towers are expected to leave at any moment. This is the most exciting moment of my life— if it passes without harm it shall be the most joyous—perhaps by tomorrow for us the war will be over . . . "

The thousands of American prisoners at *Stalag Luft* III, Sagan, Germany, were hurriedly marched from their camp on 27 January and, following a stop at Spremberg, were relocated days later in two separate camps, *Stalag* 7A at Moosburg and *Stalag* 13D at Nurnberg. On 3 April the prisoners at Nurnberg were again moved by the Germans and marched to the Moosburg camp, arriving on 20 April. The aviators were liberated by advancing American forces on 29 April following a fire fight outside the camp that raged for more than two hours.

Many of the men made sure they took their *Wartime Log* books with them, because, as one aviator said, "It was the only thing [they] had." Others were less fortunate. Some, completely exhausted from marching in sub-freezing temperatures, discarded the books along the roadside to relieve themselves of the added weight. They tore pages of the books and tossed them into open fires for added warmth.

The *Stalag Luft* III prisoners walked approximately eighty kilometers to Spremberg in frigid weather before being moved in equally cold railroad freight cars to Moosburg or Nurnberg. Capt. Thomas C. Griffin, who, like Col. C. Ross Greening, had been a participant in the 1942 raid on Tokyo, carried his *Wartime Log* book during the march from Sagan. When the prisoners arrived at Muskau, Germany, they were allowed a thirty-hour rest, during which the officer documented the experience on three pages of his book under the heading "Our Evacuation before the Russians." He wrote:

"I am writing this while lying on the cement floor of a factory in Muskau, Germany. Almost half of the officers & men of the South Compound *Stalag Luft* III are here with me. The rest of the 2000 are in another factory 1/4 mile from here. We are crowded together under our 1 Red + [Red Cross] blanket and jackets, etc. trying to get warm or preparing sandwiches & Nescafe to eat on our allotted 1/4 blanket space.

"This is Monday night. On Saturday nite we

Prisoners were preoccupied with thoughts of liberation. B-17 copilot Patrick Reams's cartoon shows his frustration over the wait.

were given 1/2 hours to abandon our prison camp [*Stalag Luft* III]. We packed as we could in our improvised packs and at 10 o'clock marched out of camp. We marched continually until 12 noon the next day except for a 1-1/2 hr. stop at about 4 o'clock during which the Germans distributed bread. We were in open country & the icy wind brought immediate chills & suffering to us. The other stops were short & often 2 hours apart. We covered 30 kilometers in this first march. Many dropped out—unable to keep up the grueling pace. Excess articles of clothing were strewn along the roads for miles as Kriegies attempted to lighten their loads.

"Our stop yesterday noon was for 4 hours in cold barns. We were packed into these so tightly we had the greatest of difficulty changing to dry sox. It was an impossibility to get comfortable, warm or rested. At four o'clock we were ordered out into ranks again. It was windy & snowing & colder than the night before. We stood in this for two hours before marching off. We started out numb & cold at six o'clock and marched for seven grueling hours, covering some 27 kilometers before reaching here. The hardships of this march were unbelievably severe—many men dropping out from sheer exhaustion and cold. We arrived here in Muskau—stood awaiting in the

(Continued)

streets for an hour—and were then permitted to enter these large, airy factory buildings. The sick were segregated and put into other factory rooms. Someone must have thought they would be warmer, but they were chilly rooms with damp cement floors, on which they had to be lain.

"It has been a tremendous rout before the Russians—full of misery for both us Kriegies [prisoners] and our German guards. Tonite rumor has it that three of them deserted. They are elderly men and for them the march must have been excruciating punishment. A favorite story that went around today was about one of our Sergeants who carried the gun of one exhausted guard so he could keep up. The old fellow had taken to crying and saying he had to keep up but he just couldn't, and wouldn't we please help him.

"We have just learned (8:00) that we have 30 more kilometers to go to some kind of destination. Col. Goodrich refused to allow the Germans to march us today and we have rested. Tomorrow we start again at about 8:00 A.M.

"Sunday, six days later: (Prison Camp 25 km N.E. Munich). We marched 18 kilos. the next day to stop that night in barns on the way. The next day we finished our march to Spremberg. At 7:00 P.M. we boarded freight cars (50 to 55 in each small car). We rode for three nights and two days over Germany's war-harried rail system to reach this camp. We were packed in so tightly over this period that it was impossible to stretch out and rest. Luckily, only once were we in a marshaling yard when the air raid sirens sounded, and then no bombs were dropped. Thank God the trip is over!"

And then, on two additional pages, Captain
(Continued)

American aviators, liberated at *Stalag* **7A, Moosburg, prepare a meal from a Red Cross food parcel. The men, who were originally imprisoned in** *Stalag Luft* **4, were liberated by American troops.** (COURTESY DANIEL WILKERSON)

BARTH

HARD TIMES

Vol 1　No. 1　LAST 1　SATURDAY MAY 5th 1945　PRICE 1 D· BAR

Editor: F'L E. R. INKPEN　　Assoc: 1st Lt N. GIDDINGS　　Publisher: 1st Lt D. MacDONALD　　Printing: F LT J. D. WHITE

RUSSKY COME!

As seen by LOWELL BENNET, I. N. S. War Correspondent.

RELIEVED!

Colonel Zemke intended to write this appreciation of the relief of Stalag Luft I, but unfortunately necessary duties have made this impossible. He has, in his own words, "taken a powder" to make final arrangements with the relieving Soviet forces.

It is therefore my privilege to introduce this Memorial Edition of the BARTH HARD TIMES.

During the successes, reverses and stagnant periods encountered during this struggle, our newspaper has faithfully recorded the German war communiqués and expanded upon them in capable editorials.

With the redemption of a continent, our exile is ended. Our, barbbound community will soon be a memory. So, on behalf of Colonel Hubert Zemke and myself, to all our fellow-kriegies: G O O D L U C K !

G. .C. C. T. Weir.

WHAT D'YE KNOW· JOE!!

BRAITHWAITE FINDS UNCLE JOE

Contacts Russian Infantryman at Crossroads
Five miles South of Stalag One.

Major Braithwaite and Sgt Korson, our Stalag scouts, raced out to a cross-roads 5 miles south of Barth with the order, "find Uncle Joe". This was 8 p. m., May 1.

They searched southward, defying a rumored Russian curfew which was about as brief and emphatic as their own order: "EVERYONE stay put; anyone seen moving will be shot on sight."

Meanwhile, Wing Commander Blackburn's telephone crew were ringing numbers in Stralsund, hoping a Russian would answer the phone and we could brea the big news of our presence. "Try th mayor," they asked the girl (who was sti working Barth's phone exchange). "No a chance," said she. "Barth's mayor pois oned himself and Stralsund's mayor ha sprouted wings."

Scouts Braithwaite and Korson pushe on 3 miles. The scenery: thousands o people everywhere, sitting down, waitin

Griffin recorded the following under the heading "Moosburg, Germany—Feb. 7, '45":

"While certain thoughts about recent events are still fairly clear in my mind I wish to jot them down. A week after our move from Stalag Luft III we have arrived at this camp 25 km. NE of Munich. It is an enlisted men's camp, containing men of every European nationality, plus Indians, So. Africans, Australians, etc. We have been crowded some 400 in each of six barracks. There is one pump and one water spigot in each barracks. What with the general dirt and crowded conditions life is quite rough. However, now at the beginning, it is a relief from the ordeal we have passed thru in arriving here. We were given hot showers (when will we get another?) our clothing was fumigated, and finally we were fed hot soup! We are now to be issued one Red Cross parcel for every three men. Everything being comparative, life is now at least bearable. There is nothing to read, no room to walk anywhere within the narrow confines of our barbed-wire fences—nothing to do but sit and wait for the war to end. There is a rumor that we may move to a camp at Nurnberg (NW of Munich) but nothing definite is known.

"Feb. 9—We are being issued 1/2 parcel of Red Cross food per man each week. The Germans give us so little coal we can barely warm our food—the barracks themselves must remain continually cold and damp. Many men have colds and stomach trouble. Many of our people have been returned who jumped off the train on the way. Our news is very spotty—but from the little we do get the west front is opening up now to augment the great Russian drive. The eternal question with us is, 'when will the Germans give up?' The eternal subject of conversation is what we will eat when we get home. Most of us agree that it is a miracle that so many of our people were able to get here. The physical stamina of the average Kriegie was remarkable. It had to be to

get him through that week. I am now wondering how to wash my clothes—let alone myself. The little water available from our spigot and pump is cold, of course, and with no receptacles the job will be hard to do. We trade cigarettes for necessities.

"Feb. 11—We have been doing our water-heating, etc., in little 'KLIM tin stoves', due to the shortage of fuel. These cans burn cardboard or wood-chips and are our only means of getting hot food.

"Apr. 9—Still kicking around. In tents—still at Moosburg. We are crowded together—several thousand officers in a small lager [camp]. There are 270 of us in this tent. One-fourth of the number would make a nice full tent. Cooking facilities—practically nil. People from all over Germany—and Poland [Shuben]—are being sent to this camp. Some came in last night from a camp near Frankfurt which was taken by an American spear-head and then re-captured by the Germans. People from Shuben were marched 48 days. The Red + has gotten food thru to us here at Moosburg. We were off parcels and on slim German rations (our dark ages—March). Despite rumors and occasionally 1/2 parcel days we are now on full Red + parcels, German rations are cut to a low figure."

Thus ends the *Wartime Log* entries concerning the captivity of Captain Thomas C. Griffin, who was liberated 29 April 1945. For him it had been a long stay—almost two years—behind the barbed wire of two German prisons. Penciled on one page near the front of the book is an entry made shortly after the officer first became a prisoner. It has as much meaning today as it did a half-century ago. The officer wrote:

God of the hidden purpose
Let our embarking be
The prayer of proud men asking
Not to be safe, but free.

Propaganda leaflets were used extensively by both the Germans and the Allies. A German leaflet addressed to captured British and American soldiers asked the prisoners to join arms with the Germans in the fight against "Bolshevik-Communism." Allied leaflets, printed with the names Churchill, Truman, and Stalin, were distributed in the final days of the war to German prison camp officials. The text offers a stern warning—anyone harming prisoners of war will be severely punished.

(COURTESY THOMAS C. GRIFFIN)

Soldiers of the British Commonwealth!
Soldiers of the United States of America!

The great Bolshevik offensive has now crossed the frontiers of Germany. The men in the Moscow Kremlin believe the way is open for the conquest of the Western world. This will certainly be the decisive battle for us. But it will also be the decisive battle for England, for the United States and for the maintenance of Western civilisation.

Or whatever today remains of it.

The events in the Baltic States, in Poland, Hungary and Greece are proof enough for us all to see the real program behind the mask of Moscow's socalled **"limited national aims"** and reveals to us how Moscow interprets democratic principles both for the countries she has conquered and also for Germany and **for your countries as well.**

It is also clear enough **today** that the issue at stake is not merely the destruction of Germany and the extermination of the German race. **The fate of your country too is at stake.** This means the fate of your wives, of your children, your home. It also means everything that make life livable, lovable and honorable for you.

Each one of you who has watched the development of Bolshevism throughout this war knows in his innermost heart the truth about Bolshevism. Therefore we are now addressing you as white men to other white men. This is not an appeal. At least we feel there is no alternative for any of us, who feels himself a citizen of our continent and our civilisation but to stop the red flood here and now.

Extraordinary events demand extraordinary measures and decisions. One of these decisions is now put up to you. We address ourselves to you regardless of your rank or of your nationality.

Soldiers! We are sure there are some amongst you who have recognized the danger of Bolshevik-Communism for his own country. We are sure that many of you have seen clearly what this war is now leading to. **We are sure that many of you see what the consequences of the destruction of Europe — not just of Germany but of Europe — will mean to your own country.** Therefore we want to make the following proposal to all of you.

We think that our fight has also become your fight. If there are some amongst you who are willing to take consequences and who are willing to join the ranks of the German soldiers who fight in this [...] fate of Germany and the fate of your countries we should like to [...] ranks and the tens of thousands of volunteers from the communist [...] eastern Europe, which have had to choose between submission under [...] a national existence in the future under European ideas, many of [...]

[...] in the front-line or in the service corps: we make you this solemn [...] is own nation is willing to join the common front for the common [...] er the victory of the present offensive and can return to his own [...]

[...] is the word of the gentleman not to fight directly or indirectly for [...] o long as this war continues.

[...] to think about Germany. We ask you to think about your own [...] e the chances which you and your people at home would have to, [...] onslaught should overpower Europe. We must and we will put [...] chieve this under all circumstances. Please inform the convoy-officer [...] ve the privileges of our own men for we expect you to share their [...] sses all national boundaries. The world today is confronted by the [...] We ask you to think it over.

[...]re of West or the barbaric asiatic East?

[...]ecision now!

Alliierte Kriegsgefangene

WARNUNG AN JEDEN, DER FÜR IHRE BEHANDLUNG VERANTWORTLICH IST

DIE Regierung von Grossbritannien, die Regierung der Vereinigten Staaten und die Regierung der Sowjet-Union richten hiermit zugleich im Namen aller Vereinten Nationen, die sich im Kriege mit Deutschland befinden, eine feierliche Warnung an alle Kommandanten und Bewachungsmannschaften, die Befehlsgewalt über alliierte Kriegsgefangene in Deutschland oder im deutschbesetzten Gebiet haben, sowie an alle Angehörigen der Geheimen Staatspolizei und an alle anderen Personen, gleichgültig welchen Dienstzweiges und welchen Ranges, die alliierte Kriegsgefangene in Händen haben, sei es im Kampfgebiet, auf den Verbindungswegen oder im rückwärtigen Gebiet. Sie erklären hiermit, dass sie alle diese Personen ebenso wie das deutsche Oberkommando und die zuständigen deutschen Heeres-, Kriegsmarine- und Luftwaffe- Behörden für die Sicherheit und Wohlfahrt der ihnen anvertrauten alliierten Kriegsgefangenen persönlich verantwortlich machen.

Jedermann, der alliierte Kriegsgefangene misshandelt oder solche Misshandlung zulässt, gleichgültig ob im Kampfgebiet, auf den Verbindungswegen, im Lager, Lazarett, Gefängnis oder wo auch immer, wird rücksichtslos verfolgt und seiner Bestrafung zugeführt werden.

Sie weisen darauf hin, dass sie diese Verantwortung unter allen Umständen als bindend betrachten; auch kann diese Verantwortung nicht auf irgendwelche anderen Behörden oder Einzelpersonen abgeschoben werden.

Winston Churchill   *Harry S. Truman*   *Josef Stalin*

A FRIENDLIER SPOTLIGHT

New York City's colorful mayor, Fiorello H. LaGuardia, clutched an odd-looking cutting tool during the opening of a special exhibition at New York City's Museum of Science and Industry. With a snapping sound, he cut the ceremonial piece of barbed wire, officially opening the "Army Air Force P.O.W. Exposition." The instrument he used to cut the wire had been fashioned out of ice skate blades by a prisoner of war who designed the tool to cut the barbed wire surrounding his camp.

The date was 1 October 1945, just months after the end of World War II. The exposition, organized by Col. Charles Ross Greening, noted artist of *Stalag Luft* I, was on the first leg of a tour that would take approximately eight hundred handmade artifacts, including artwork drawn and painted by American prisoners in *Wartime Log* books, to major cities throughout the United States. The goal of the exhibit was to show the public how American prisoners of war in Europe, and specifically those airmen in *Stalag Luft* I, had used creativity and American ingenuity to survive their prison camp environment.

The setting for this unique exhibition was indeed ironic. The museum opened in 1936 to showcase advancements in science and industry. Dr. Albert Einstein was among those present at the dedication. According to the *New York Times*

account published 12 February 1936, Einstein urged wider dissemination of knowledge so that all people could learn.

"There is one advantage which primitive man has over civilized man," Einstein said at the dedication. "He is acquainted with the primitive tools which he is using; he can make his own bow and arrow, in fact, even his own canoe. How many of the civilized people have to any extent a clear idea about the nature and origin of the things the use or consumption of which he takes so much as a matter of course?"

During the opening of the prisoner of war exposition, Mayor LaGuardia seemed amazed at the accomplishments of those who had created so much using so little. During World War I, the mayor had served in the American air service as a pilot-bombardier on the Italian-Austrian front. He no doubt felt a kinship to these fellow aviators. What was intended to be a very brief visit to participate in the ribbon-cutting became an intense two-hour tour.

Violinist Carol Glenn, wife of musician Eugene List, was asked to play the violin made by prisoner Claire Cline. Mayor LaGuardia watched and listened intently as music filled the hall.

The "Army Air Force P.O.W. Exposition" spread the story of these brave and ingenious airmen.

New York City Mayor Fiorello H. LaGuardia cuts the barbed wire to open the "Army Air Force P.O.W. Exposition" at the Museum of Science and Industry. Exhibit organizer Col. C. Ross Greening watches at center and fellow prisoner of war Al Ricci, who took art lessons from the colonel while at *Stalag Luft* I, watches at far right.

Carol Glenn plays prisoner of war Claire Cline's violin at the exhibit opening while Mayor LaGuardia and Colonel Greening watch.

(COURTESY DOROTHY FISHBURNE)

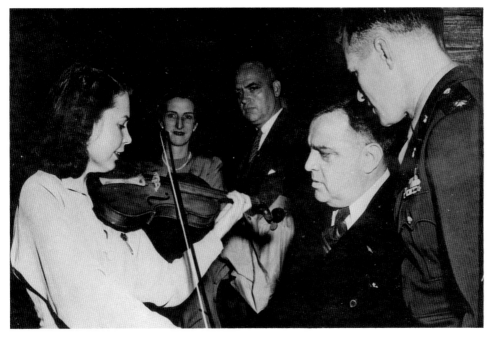

THE TOUR

Newspaper ads promoted the "Army Air Force P.O.W. Exposition" in cities throughout the United States. This full-page ad ran in Chicago prior to the exhibit's opening at Marshall Field & Company on 11 March 1946.

(COURTESY DOROTHY FISHBURNE)

From 1 October 1945, when the "Army Air Force P.O.W. Exposition" opened at the Museum of Science and Industry in New York, to mid-September 1946, the exhibit of prisoner-made artifacts was displayed in major American cities. More than four million Americans viewed the exhibition.

Colonel Greening and his staff arranged to show the artifacts in department stores because they were accessible to the general public. Information officers promoted the exposition in the local news media.

The tour included: Boston, Massachusetts (Filene's Department Store), 17-27 January; Utica, New York (J.B. Wells & Son), 4-10 February; Cleveland, Ohio (The Higbee Co.), 18-23 February; Columbus, Ohio (F. & R. Lazarus Co.), 27 February-5 March; Chicago, Illinois (Marshall Field & Co.), 11-23 March; Minneapolis, Minnesota (Baker Co.), 29 March-8 April; Des Moines, Iowa (Younkers Brothers), 11-24 April; Omaha, Nebraska (Orchard & Wilhelm Co.), 29 April-4 May; Denver, Colorado (The May Co.), 11-18 May; Spokane, Washington (Tull & Gibbs Store), 3-11 June; San Francisco, California (J.C. Penny Co.), 20 June-3 July; Los Angeles, California (Millirons 5th Street Store), 10-23 July; Salt Lake City, Utah (Z.C.M.I. Store), 30 July-12 August; Dallas, Texas (Titche-Goettinger Co.), 23 August-6 September; and Washington, D.C. (Lansburgh's Department Store), 16-21 September.

After the tour most of the artwork and handicrafts were moved to the United States Air Force Museum at Wright-Patterson Air Force Base, in Dayton, Ohio, where the artifacts are still on display.

This exhibit of American ingenuity remains one of the most popular at the United States Air Force Museum, just as it was half a century ago.

16 MAN ROOM

The exhibition provided a look at a typical barracks room (sometimes occupied by as many as sixteen men) and a variety of cooking equipment. It also featured a re-creation of a typical prison camp solitary confinement cell.

(COURTESY DOROTHY FISHBURNE)

EPILOGUE

As you sat and read this book
With its faces so breezy
I know damn well just what you thought
"By God they had it easy."
 One second friend, before you speak
 Just listen to this story
 Of pain from out a Kriegie's life
 Filled with static glory.
My grazing ground is one square mile
Encircled by barbed wire fences
Here and there a guard box tall
And the guards aren't armed with lances.
 It measures only five by five
 The men are six feet tall
 Put ten of them into this room
 There ain't no room at all.
We rest amid our many dreams
Of days before we fell
And just when we are dozing off
We hear that damn appel.

Ten hungry men, how they can eat
For meat they rave and cry
But in the Reich there ain't no meat
 On spuds we must get by.
Their faces filled, their fags all lit
They jump upon their sacks
But still remain the dirty dishes
I wash; the guys make cracks.
 A favorite cry around the camp
 From inmates of this jail
 "My God" they say, "this makes ten months
 And still I've got no mail!"
I've read about our lovely camp
In the Red Cross paper
"Your swimming pool, extended trips
I know they meet your favor."
 It's this they write in all my mail
 All this bull and hokum
 The thing they just can't realize
 is "Alles ist Verboten."

— FROM CLAUDIUS BELK'S *WARTIME LOG*
(COURTESY NORM FLAYDERMAN)

Two hundred and two American P.O.W.s from all branches of service died in the European and Mediterranean theaters during World War II. Prisoners bravely faced death every day. Accident, illness, enemy small arms fire, and Allied bombs were just some of the threats. The cause of death and identity of this American aviator imprisoned at *Stalag Luft* III were not recorded with these photos, which are from the American Red Cross Archives. Fellow prisoners are shown standing at attention during the funeral procession. At the grave a comrade holds a small American flag while a German camp official places a wreath to honor the fallen airman. For this man, prison camp was the final mission.

(COURTESY AMERICAN RED CROSS)

APPENDIX

The following reports are located in the American Red Cross archives, Washington, D.C. Only those parts of the reports which deal with Army Air Force P.O.W.s are reprinted in this appendix.

AMERICAN PRISONERS OF WAR IN GERMANY

Prepared by Military Intelligence Service War Department
1 November 1945

Introduction

Conditions in German prisoner of war camps holding Americans varied to such an extent that only by examination of individual camps can a clear picture be drawn. This report contains summaries of 12 typical German installations ranging from Stalag Luft 3, a well organized camp for Air Force officers, through Stalag 2B, an average Ground Force enlisted men's camp, to chaotic Stalag 9B, established for enlisted men captured during the Von Rundstadt offensive of December 1944.

Germany held a total of 92,965★ American prisoners of war in these categories:

Air Forces	32,730
Ground Forces	60,235

In contrast to the number of Ground Force officers who formed only some 10% of the Ground Force prisoners of war, almost 50% of the Air Force personnel falling into enemy hands were officers. Figures for both branches soared during the 10 months after 6 June 1944 when totals were:

Air Forces	15,093
Ground Forces	9,274
Total	24,367

For army prisoners of war, Germany had three principal types of camp. OFLAG, a contraction of *Offizier Lager* (officers' camp), as its title denotes held officers. STALAG, a contraction of *Stamm Lager* (main camp) held enlisted men. DULAG, a contraction of *Durchgangs Lager* (entrance camp) was a transit camp but in the minds of airmen became synonymous with interrogation center. LUFT (air) appended to a name indicated that the camp held flying personnel. Generally, camps housing airmen were under the jurisdiction of the Luftwaffe, and camps housing ground troops under the jurisdiction of the Wehrmacht.

Prisoners of war (PW) formed camps within camps and had their own organizations. In officers' camps they were headed by the Senior American Officer (SAO) who was just what his name implied. In enlisted men's stalags, the Man of Confidence (MOC) was usually an NCO elected by his fellow PW, but sometimes he was appointed by the Germans.

Source material for this report consisted of interrogations of former prisoners of war made by CPM Branch, Military Intelligence Service, and reports of the Protecting Power and International Red Cross received by the State Department (Special War Problems Division).

DULAG LUFT

Introduction

Dulag Luft, through which practically all air force personnel captured in German-occupied Europe passed, was composed of three installations: the interrogation center at Oberursel, the hospital at Hohemark and the transit camp ultimately at Wetzlar.

INTERROGATION CENTER

Location

Auswertestelle West (Evaluation Center West) was situated 300 yards north of the main Frankfurt-Homburg road and near the trolley stop of Kupforhammer - the third stop after Oberursel (50° 12' N. - 8° 34" E). Oberursel is 13 kilometers northwest of Frankfurt-on-Main.

Strength

The number of PW handled rose from 1000 a month in late 1943 to an average monthly intake of 2000 in 1944. The peak month was July 1944 when over 3000 Allied airmen and paratroopers passed through Auswertestelle West. Since solitary confinement was the rule, the capacity of the camp was sup-

★1 Nov. 45 Records

posedly limited to 200 men, although in rush periods as many as five PW were placed in one cell. Strength on any given day averaged 250.

Description

The main part of the camp consisted of four large wooden barracks two of which, connected by a passage and known to PW as the "cooler," contained some 200 cells. These cells, eight feet high, five feet wide and 12 feet long held a cot, a table, a chair and an electric bell for PW to call the guard. The third barrack contained administrative headquarters. The fourth building, a large "L" shaped structure, housed the interrogating offices, files and records. Senior officers lived on the post; junior officers outside in a hotel. The commandant lived on a nearby farm. The entire camp was surrounded by a barbed-wire fence but was equipped with neither perimeter floodlights nor watchtowers.

U.S. Personnel

Since PW were held in solitary confinement, and only for limited periods of time, no U.S. staff existed.

German Personnel

German personnel - all Luftwaffe - was divided into two main branches: Administrative and Intelligence. Under Intelligence came officers and interpreter NCOs actually taking part in the interrogations and other intelligence work of the unit. The total strength of this branch was 50 officers and 100 enlisted men. Administrative personnel consisted of one guard company and one Luftwaffe construction company, each consisting of 120 men. Some members of the staff were:

Oberstleutnant Erich Killinger: Commandant
Major Junge: Chief of Interrogation
Major Boehringer: Executive Officer
Captain Schneidewindt: Record Section Chief
Leutnant Böninghaus: Political Interrogator

Later there were attached to the staff representatives of the General Luftzeugmeister's department, the General der Kampfflieger's section, the Navy and the S.S. Occasionally members of the Gestapo at Frankfurt were permitted to interrogate PW.

Treatment

The interrogation of Allied PW at the hands of Auswertestelle West personnel was "korrect" as far as physical violence was concerned. An occasional interrogator, exasperated by polite refusals to give more than name, rank, serial number or, more occasionally,

perhaps by an exceptionally "fresh" PW, may have lost his temper and struck a PW. It is not believed that this ever went beyond a slap on the face dealt in the heat of anger - certainly physical violence was not employed as a policy. On the other hand, no amount of calculated mental depression, privation and psychological blackmail was considered excessive.

Upon arrival, PW were stripped, searched, and sometimes issued German coveralls. At other times they retained the clothing in which they were shot down. All were shut up in solitary confinement cells and denied cigarettes, toilet articles and Red Cross food. Usually the period of confinement lasted four or five days, but occasionally a surly PW would be held in the "cooler" for the full 30 days permitted by the Geneva Convention as a punitive measure, and Captain William N. Schwartz was imprisoned 45 days. Interrogators often used threats and violent language, calling PW "murderers of children" and threatening them with indefinitely prolonged solitary confinement on starvation rations unless they would talk. PW were threatened with death as spies unless they identified themselves as airmen by revealing technical information on some such subject as radar or air combat tactics. Confinement in an unbearably overheated cell and pretended shootings of "buddies" were resorted to in the early days. Intimidation yielded inferior results and the friendly approach was considered best by the Germans.

Food

Rations were two slices of black bread and jam with ersatz coffee in the morning, watery soup at midday, two slices of bread at night. No Red Cross parcels were issued. PW could obtain drinking water from the guards.

Health

As a rule, men seriously needing medical treatment were sent to Hohemark hospital. Those suffering from the shock of being shot down and captured received no medical attention, nor did the 50% suffering from minor wounds. Some PW arrived at permanent camps still wearing dirty bandages which had not been changed at Oberursel even though their stay had been of two weeks' duration. Upon several occasions PW were denied the ministration of either a doctor or medical orderly and there is at least one instance where a flyer with a broken leg was refused treatment of any sort until he had answered some of the interrogator's questions four days after his arrival.

Clothing

PW received no Red Cross clothing. Instead they

wore German fatigues or the uniforms in which they had been captured - minus leather jackets which were customarily confiscated.

Work   None

Pay   None

Mail   None

Morale

There is little doubt that the living conditions were expressly designed to lower morale and to produce mental depression of the most acute kind. Still, due partially to briefings which acquainted them with Oberursel and partially to their innate sense of loyalty, most PW successfully withstood the harsh treatment and yielded no important military information other than name, rank and serial number.

Welfare

Neither the Protecting Power, which was refused admission for a long time, nor the Red Cross nor the YMCA could do anything to ameliorate the condition of PW in the interrogation center.

Religion   None

Recreation   None

Liberation

On 25 April 1945 American troops overran Oberursel. They found Auswertestelle West no longer a going concern. Some 10 days earlier, its departments already widely dispersed over what remained of Germany, the installation had ceased to exist even as a headquarters of the German Air Interrogation service. Its records had been burnt or evacuated and its leading personalities, taking with them what remained of their organization, had fled to a new site at Nurnberg-Buchenbuhl. The new Dulag headquarters at Nurnberg did not survive the parent unit by many days. It was not long before Oberstleutnant Erich Killinger, the commandant, was discovered by Allied interrogators in an army cage. With the former roles of captive and interrogator now so completely reversed, it was a slightly apprehensive but stubborn Killinger who accompanied his captors back to the scene of his former triumphs at Oberursel.

HOHEMARK HOSPITAL

As soon as the Luftwaffe took over the Oberursel installation in December 1939 it became obvious that a high percentage of PW would be in need of medical attention. To meet this, the camp authorities requisitioned part of Hohemark hospital one mile west of the interrogation center. This hospital had been used since World War I as a health resort and clinic for all types of brain injuries and contained a large number of German soldiers wounded in this war.

The wards for PW were on the second floor and comprised one single room, two double rooms and several rooms with four beds, totaling 65. Discipline was very mild. The doors of the wards were not always locked at night, and the only guards were the German medical orderlies. German medical treatment was excellent, as was the food, which came from the Red Cross special invalid parcels and from the hospital kitchen. Walking cases were frequently allowed to meet and take meals together. Other ambulatory cases, as soon as their condition permitted, were allowed parole walks through the surrounding grounds and countryside.

Wounded men were sometimes interrogated directly during their stay at the hospital. At other times, they were not interrogated until after their convalescence when they were sent to Oberursel. The comparatively luxurious single and double rooms were set aside as places where high-ranking Allied PW could be interrogated in circumstances which the Germans considered appropriate to their rank. These PW did not have to be wounded to gain admission to Hohemark.

Several British and American orderlies formed part of the hospital complement. They were headed by an Edward Stafford, an American who was captured while flying in the RAF Ferry Command and called himself "Captain." His assistant was Captain Kenneth Smith, who was receiving treatment for facial burns during his stay. Inmates of Hohemark received the normal allotment of outgoing letters, but only the permanent staff received incoming letters. PW's only religious activity was listening to the Bible readings of a Hauptmann Offerman.

Hohemark was liberated simultaneously with Oberursel.

TRANSIT CAMP

Location

On 10 September 1943 the Dulag Luft transit camp, where PW who had been interrogated awaited shipment to permanent stalags, was moved from

Oberursel to Frankfurt-on-Main. Here it was situated in the Palm Gardens only 1665 yards northwest of the main railroad station - a location which was a target area and therefore endangered the lives of PW.

On 15 November 1943 the Swiss stated, "This visit (to the camp) leaves a bad impression because of the new situation of the Dulag, so exposed to attacks from the air, which is not in conformity with Article 9 of the (Geneva) Convention."

Thus the following Swiss announcement in the spring of 1944 came as no surprise: "Dulag Luft, Wetzlar, is succeeding Dulag Luft, Frankfurt, which was destroyed in course of one of the latest (24 March) air raids on Frankfurt. The camp is situated on a slightly elevated position approximately three to four kilometers west north west from Wetzlar, a town some 50 kilometers north of Frankfurt-on-Main and is a former German army camp (Flak troops)."

Strength

During the first nine months of 1943, 1000 PW a month passed through the transit camp. This increased to 1500 a month, half British and half American, in the last three months of the year. Statistics for October 1944 follow:

Incoming Personnel Total 1963
Daily Average 63
Total American 1312
    Officers 155
    NCOs 739
Total British. 651
    Officers 155
    NCOs 496

Camp strength fluctuated from day to day. On the Swiss visit of 10 November 1944 it was 311; on 13 March 1945 it was 826. Except for the permanent staff of 30, PW seldom stayed more than eight days.

Description

During May and June 1944, inmates lived in 18 tents pitched on the eastern side of the camp area. On 13 July 1944, they moved to the newly-constructed buildings: five barracks and one large bungalow which held the messes and the store rooms. Capacity of the camp was 784, with tents available in case of a sudden influx. Two of the sleeping barracks were reserved for officers, two for NCOs, and the remaining one accommodated the permanent camp staff, sick rooms and medical inspection room. The mess had space for 300 men in the main room. The camp staff, the officers and the enlisted men ate separately.

Each room in the barracks held six to eight triple-decker bunks - 18 to 24 men. Each bed had a mattress filled with wood shavings and one pillow. All barracks had special wash rooms with built-in basins and running cold water.

Unoccupied space within the barbed wire was somewhat limited after the erection of the last two barracks and the laying out of vegetable gardens cultivated for and by the PW. The area gave a neat appearance, however, with tidy paths and well-tended lawns.

U.S. Personnel

Senior Allied Officer at Wetzlar was Colonel Charles W. Stark who enjoyed exceptionally friendly terms with the Germans and drew many concessions from them. Members of his staff were:

1st Lt. Gerald G. Gille: Adjutant
2nd Lt. Arthur C. Jaros: Adjutant
2nd Lt. Herbert Schubert: Mess Officer

In addition, the staff comprised:
1 Chaplain
5 Kitchen orderlies
4 Mess orderlies
5 Store orderlies
4 Barracks chiefs
3 Medical orderlies
4 Barracks orderlies
1 Gardener
1 Carpenter

A previous Senior American Officer was 1st Lt. John G. Winant.

German Personnel

The housekeeping organization consisted of:

Oberstleutnant Becker: Commandant
Major Hiess: Camp Officer
Major Salzar: Camp Officer
Major Heyden: Camp Officer
Dr. Thomai: Medical Officer
Dr. Wenger: Medical Officer
Hauptmann Schmid: Security Officer

In November 1944 there was reported the existence at the camp of an interrogation center. According to Colonel Stark, treatment was good and correct in every way. Some PW arriving from Oberursel were in solitary and asked purely "political" questions for two or three days. Then they were admitted to the transit camp. Chief of this interrogation section was Major Ernst Dornseifer.

Treatment

Treatment was better here than at any other American PW camp in Germany. German and American staffs seemed to cooperate with each other, resulting in favorable living conditions to both parties. The Senior Allied Officer operated Wetzlar as a rest camp where PW suffering from the harsh treatment at Oberursel might regain their strength and morale before traveling to permanent camps. As a result neither Germans nor Americans provoked any untoward incidents.

Food

No food shortage existed at Wetzlar, even though the Germans repeatedly cut their ration until the daily issue per man was officially announced in March 1945 as:

Meat	35 grams
Potatoes	320 grams
Margarine	31 grams
Butter	25 grams
Sugar	25 grams
Bread	75 grams
Salt	20 grams
Coffee (ersatz)	5 grams

For three days:

Barley	10 grams
Millet	21 grams
Hulsenfruchte	63 grams
Cheese	14 grams
White Cheese	14 grams

The difference between this sub-sustenance diet and the good meals actually eaten by PW was made up by Red Cross food. One parcel per PW was drawn each week and 90% of all Red Cross food was given to the kitchen to improve German rations. Usually the stock on hand consisted of four months' supply. Even in September 1944 when the order was given to cut food reserves to a very minimum, Wetzlar authorities allowed PW to keep four weeks' supply on hand. In March 1945, anticipating a possible evacuation from Wetzlar to the interior of the Reich, the SAO authorized the issue of two Red Cross food parcels per man per week, both to strengthen PW for the march to come and to prevent the loss of food which would be abandoned in the event of a sudden move.

The kitchen - staffed by Americans - was well equipped with two large cooking ranges, three boilers, a dish-washing room, a potato-peeling room, a tin-opening room and an adjacent storeroom.

Health

The sick bays were able to accommodate 40 men in beds, two of which were in a separate room reserved for contagious diseases. The medical inspection room was described as adequate and all necessary medicines and instruments were made available either from Red Cross sources or - to a lesser extent - from the Germans. Good medical treatment was received from the German staff doctor who cooperated first with Lt. Anthony S. Barling, RAMC, and then with Captain Peter Griffin during their brief stays in camp.

Each man received a hot shower upon his entrance to the compound and was subsequently permitted to take one each week. Although the barracks washroom taps ran only cold water, hot water could usually be drawn elsewhere some hours during the day. A 10-seat outdoor latrine was supplemented by satisfactory toilets of the modern flush type.

Although many men arriving from Oberursel were wounded and exhausted, the general state of health was considered good.

Clothing

Large numbers of PW arrived without outer uniforms, and sometimes without underclothing or shoes. Each new arrival was equipped with at least the following articles - all of which were supplied not by the Germans but by the Red Cross:

1 shirt	1 necktie
1 pr. drawers	1 pr. trousers
1 undershirt	1 blouse
1 pr. socks	1 pr. shoes
1 set toilet articles	

Initially, the shortage of American stocks necessitated the drawing of British clothing. Later, however, most of the clothing issued was of American origin, and eventually it was possible to keep adequate stocks of British and American items separately. In March 1945 it was no longer possible to provide PW with neatly packed "captive cases" a sort of suitcase containing the articles listed above, for the supply was exhausted.

Work

Since air force personnel consisted solely of commissioned and non-commissioned officers, no work beyond some of their own housekeeping chores were [sic] required of them.

Pay

PW received no pay, but when the camp opened in the summer of 1944, the finance committee of Stalag Luft 3, Sagan, sent the permanent staff a fund of over 4000 reichmarks.

Mail

Transients were allowed to send their first letter or a postcard form informing next-of-kin of their status and address, but received no incoming mail. The permanent staff drew the usual allotment of letter forms and received incoming mail as well. Some air mail from the United States was received within three weeks. Average time for both air and surface mail was four months. As with all Luftwaffe camps, letters were censored at Sagan.

Morale

The Senior Allied Officer agreed with statements of the Swiss Delegates and German camp authorities that Wetzlar was an excellent camp and that "such favorable conditions are hardly to be found elsewhere in Germany." Morale of men leaving Oberursel was usually at its lowest ebb, and it is small wonder after receiving food, clothing and mingling in comparative freedom with their fellow Americans, that their spirits soared back to a level approaching normality. Most of them left Wetzlar prepared to face the difficulties of their new lives as PW.

Welfare

The Protecting Power visited Wetzlar in May, July, November 1944 and March 1945 - each time forwarding the complaints of the Senior Allied Officer and making a complete report on camp conditions.

The Red Cross supplied PW with practically all their food, clothing and medical supplies but made no visit until January 1945, when they wrote a report of their inspection.

From the YMCA, the camp received most of its library, which eventually totaled 1500 books, and equipment for indoor games and outdoor sports.

Religion

For some months the only religious activity was the regular Sunday service conducted by Warrant Officer Hooton, RAF, a Methodist. Early in 1945 Captain Daniel McGowan, a Catholic priest, conducted both Catholic and Protestant services every Sunday.

Recreation

New arrivals were usually in such condition as not to want strenuous exercise. Games, therefore, were as a rule limited to milder sports such as deck tennis. Once a week some PW were permitted walks outside the camp. The most popular indoor pastimes were reading, playing cards, discussing the new experience of being a PW and playing some of the table games provided by the YMCA.

Evacuation & Liberation

The Wetzlar camp log from 27 through 30 March follows:

27 March 1945

0530 German order to evacuate all those able to walk with the exception of few permanent staff, who should remain to run the place. 143 remained including Col. Stark, Lt. Jaros, Lt. Comdr. Jennings, Capt. Griffin, Lt. Gille and Capt. Rev. McGowan. German personnel left were 107 men, 34 women, including Maj. Dornseifer, Lt. Weyrich, and Mr. Rickmers.

0730 Transport left (82 men)

0830 We hear gun fire and sounds of approaching vehicles. Germans from across the road move into our shelters.

0945 Hear our troops are 4 kms west of us. Heavy gun fire all around.

1030 Heavy firing continues all around us. German guards are voluntarily laying down their arms.

1200 Col. Stark calls Mr. Rickmers and Lt. Weyrich into office and states that all guards turn in weapons and a system of joint sentry duty be posted. They agree and he is now in command - Maj. Dornseifer cooperating fully in this.

1430 Activity has been heavy all around us all afternoon.

1700 Fairly quiet for the moment. Col. ordered two privates to be put in the guard house cells as they are obviously drunk. German guards brought liquor into camp. He has issued orders for no drinking including the Germans.

2030 Col. sent F/Lt. Lyons, Sgt. Hanson and Mr. Rickmers to try contacting our forces in the west and report our location.

2300 Still very active all around us - M.G. fire and artillery.

2400 Still a good deal of firing. Most of the personnel sleep in shelters.

28 March 1945

0630 Fairly constant gun fire and activity all night.

1000 Dr. Griffin takes wounded Pfc. into Wetzlar for operation. Armored column passing to east of us.

1200 Lt. Valentine arrives in jeep. Boy, are we happy to see a Yank!

1500 Col. Stark and Capt. Griffin are off to staff HQ with Lt. Valentine.

1700 Sgt. Hanson and Mr. Rickmers return. There has been heavy firing around us all day.

1800 German paratroopers walk into camp and surrender. They are locked up.

1830 Col. Stark returns with 3 War News Correspondents including Belden.

2400 Things are fairly quiet.

29 March 1945

0940 Spot cub plane landed on play field.

0945 Dogs were shot.

1000 Lt. Col. Grant of 7th Armored Division (?) arrived in jeep advising us of 750 PWs he had picked up. Limburg PWs are lousy and half starved. We have sent for them and will put them up here.

1200 Four Piper Cubs landed.

1300 Maj. McDougall (?), Medical Officer, arrived and will stay the afternoon in order to help with Limburg PWs.

1400 Col. Stark and party go out to recc'y some German motor equipment.

1415 Maj. Dornseifer gave Col. Stark a list of his people who he is anxious to have out of camp as they have strong party sympathies and might make trouble. Col. Stark turns them over to an Infantry Patrol. They include the following: Sgt. Lehmann, Sgt. Hackmann, Cpl. Busch, Cpl. Stoeckel and Cpl. Schaaf.

1420 First lot of distressed PWs arrived and are deloused, bathed and clothed.

1530 Maj. Teese, PWX-SHAEF executive, arrives with load of PWs.

1745 We are to be loaded with PWs. They have been arriving all PM.

2130 Finished feeding for night. 400 odd still to be deloused.

30 March 1945

Work continues thru the day, delousing and feeding PWs arriving in camp. Maj. Teese returns and advises us to expect 320 PWs from Hadamar in the morning. This lot will include 14 General officers and 79 Field Grade officers. Seven PWs return from our last transport, including W/Comdr. Carling-Kelly. Today the remaining German personnel was officially put to work in the office, on kitchen detail, policing camp, etc. They are dealt with thru Maj. Dornseifer, Mr. Rickmers and Sgt. Keller.

Work is going on to prepare for the maximum number this camp will hold. Medical officers have arrived and are organizing their departments. They hope to start evacuating the worst cases shortly. The Hadamar contingent started arriving at 1100.

With the arrival of British officers who outranked him, Col. Stark was no longer Senior Allied Officer present. Major Teese of PWX-SHAEF, suggested that the staff remain and help in processing PW expected to arrive within the next few weeks. A stay of such length did not seem necessary to Col. Stark and at 0515 in the morning of 31 March he drove away in a German car with Comdr. Jennings, USNR, and S/Sgt. Lee Hughes, AAF, leaving a note for Lt. Gille. He proceeded by motor and air transport to Paris, arriving 3 April 1945.

STALAG LUFT 1
(Air Force Officers)

Location

Stalag Luft 1 was situated at Barth, Germany, (54° 22' N - 12° 42' 30" E), a small town on the Baltic Sea 23 kilometers northwest of Stralsund.

Strength

Stalag Luft 1 was opened in October 1942 as a British camp, but when the Red Cross visited the camp in February 1943, two American non-commissioned officers had already arrived. By January 1944, 507 American air force officers were detained there. The strength of the camp grew rapidly from this date until April 1944 when the Red Cross reported 3,463 inmates. New compounds were opened and quickly filled. Nearly 6,000 PW were crowded into the camp in September 1944, and at the time of the liberation of the camp 7,717 Americans and 1,427 Britons were returned to military control.

Description

Early in 1944 the camp consisted of two compounds designated as South and West Compounds, containing a total of seven barracks in which American officers and British officers and enlisted men were housed. A new compound was opened the last of February 1944 and was assigned to the American officers who were rapidly increasing in number. This compound became North 1, and the opening of North 2 Compound on 9 September 1944 and North 3 Compound on 9 December 1944 completed the camp as it remained until 15 May 1945. The South Compound was always unsatisfactory due to the complete lack of adequate cooking, washing, and toilet facilities. The West Compound, however, provided inside latrines and running water in the barracks. North 1 Compound formerly housed personnel of the Hitler Youth, and because of its communal messhall, inside latrines, and running water taps, it was considered by far the best compound. North 2 and North 3 Compounds were constructed on the same design as the South Compound, and were as unsatisfactory.

The completion of the last two compounds gave the camp an L-shape appearance, which followed the natural contours of the bay on which the camp was situated. Guard towers were placed at strategic intervals, and although the compounds were inter-communicating the gates were closed at all times after the Spring of 1944. Prior to that, gates were kept open during the day.

Each barrack contained triple-tiered wooden beds equipped with mattresses filled with wood chips. A communal day-room was set aside in almost every barrack, but equipment was negligible. Lighting was inadequate throughout the camp, and since the Detaining Power required the shutters to remain closed from 2100 to 0600, ventilation was entirely insufficient.

In addition to the buildings for housing, North 1 and West Compounds contained 1 kitchen-barrack, 1 theater room, 1 church room, 1 library, and 1 study room each. These were used by all compounds because no other facilities were available. Maintenance of the buildings was completely lacking in spite of the fact that the officers volunteered to take care of many of the repairs if furnished the necessary equipment.

Stoves for heating and cooking varied in each compound except that facilities in all compounds were inadequate. Many of the buildings were not weather proof, and the extremely cold climate of northern Germany made living conditions more difficult for the PW.

U.S. Personnel

Major Wilson P. Todd was the Senior American Officer until 19 January 1944 when Colonel William A. Hatcher arrived and replaced him. Colonel Jean R. Byerly acted as his Executive Officer until the opening of the North 1 Compound of which he became SAO. Toward the last of February however, Colonel Hatcher protested so strongly to the Detaining Power over the poor conditions in the camp that he was suddenly transferred to Stalag Luft 3 leaving Colonel Byerly as the SAO. At that time the compounds had been run as separate camps with little coordination between the compounds. After meeting with the Senior officers of all barracks, it was

agreed that the British and Americans would be administered separately but with very close liaison, and that all Americans would be administered under a Provisional Wing Headquarters composed of four American groups. This organization was established on 6 April 1944 and remained somewhat the same until the liberation. Upon arrival of Colonel Hubert Zemke, the Provisional Wing was turned over to his command.

Several changes were made as the camp enlarged, but for the most part the camp administration was carried out on a military basis similar to the operation of an air base. At the time Colonel Byerly turned over the command to Colonel Zemke, his staff was as follows:

Captain M.W. Zahn	Adjutant
Colonel C.R. Greening	CO, Gp. 1
Colonel E.A. Malmstrom	CO, Gp. 2
Lt. Col. C. Wilson	CO, Gp. 5
Lt. Col. F.S. Gabreski	CO, Gp. 6

(Groups 3 and 4 were British groups).

Because the advance of the Russians indicated an early liberation, Colonel Zemke changed the organization to an inter-Allied wing, nominating Group Captain C.T. Weir as chief of staff of the organization called Provisional Wing X. Group commanders were retained and continued to be responsible for the administration, security, discipline and welfare of their own groups, but more emphasis was directed toward staff operations in the event of liberation. For this work, the following staff was appointed and served until the entire camp was evacuated:

Captain C.T. Weir	Chief of Staff
Captain M.W. Zahn	Adjutant
Lt. Col. C.F. McKenna	A-1
Lt. Col. L.C. McCollom	A-2
Lt. Col. J.V.G. Wilson	A-3
Lt. Col. Luther Richmond	A-4
Lt. Col. B.E. McKenzie	Provost Marshall
Major J.J. Fischer	Judge Advocate
1st Lt. J.S. Durakov	Russian Interpreter
2d Lt. T.L. Simmons	Finance Officer

Each staff officer had several assistants to aid him in the performance of his duties. There also existed a Security organization.

German Personnel

The German personnel changed frequently during the existence of the camp. The officers, their positions, and the dates that they served are listed below.

Commandant:

Oberst Sherer	Sep. 43 to Jan. 45
Oberst Warnstadt	Jan. 45 to Apr. 45

Adjutant:

Hauptmann Tems	Sep. 43 to Mar. 44
Hauptmann Erbslch	Mar. 44 to June 44
Major Buchard	June 44 to Apr. 45

Lager Officer W.

Hauptmann Eilers	Sep. 43 to Feb. 44
Hauptmann Wolf	Feb. 44 to June 44
Hauptmann von Beck	Feb. 44 to Oct. 44
Hauptmann Luckt	Oct. 44 to Jan. 45
Major Opperman	Jan. 45 to Apr. 45

Lager Officer N.1

Hauptmann Erbslch	Feb. 44 to June 44
Major Schroeder	June 44 to July 44
Haupt. von Stradiot	Jul. 44 to Oct. 44
Hauptmann Probst	Oct. 44 to Dec. 44
Major Steinhower	Dec. 44 to Apr. 45

Lager Officer N.2

Major Sprotte	Sep. 44 to Oct. 44
Major Steinhower	Oct. 44 to Dec. 44
Hauptmann Bloom	Dec. 44 to Apr. 45

Lager Officer N.3

Hauptmann Probst	Dec. 44 to Apr. 45

Of the above listed German officers, Major Opperman was the local Nazi leader and instructed the lager personnel and guards on all Nazi policies. The other outstanding members of the Nazi party were Oberst Sherer, Major Sprotte, Major von Miller, Major Schroeder, Hauptmann Erbslch and Hauptmann Tems.

Following the Normandy invasion the ardent Nazis tried to discuss the Nazi policy with the senior officers and to sway them to the German viewpoint of the war against the Russians. The Americans, nevertheless, did not enter into any discussions.

Treatment

Prior to April 1944 treatment was considered fairly good. Following the April meeting of the Protecting Power, however, the German attitude towards PW became more severe. New orders regarding air raids were issued by the Germans. These required all personnel to be inside when the "immediate warning" siren was blown. As a result, three cases of German patrol guards shooting at men inside the camp occurred during May. At the same time the Commandant issued regulations authorizing guards to use firearms to avenge what they termed "insults to German honor." The German interpretation of this order was extremely liberal, and more shooting

developed. Oberst Scherer also became more severe in confining PW to the arrest-lock for minor infractions of German disciplinary regulations. He further denied all Red Cross foods and personal parcels as well as tobacco to PW undergoing confinement in the arrest-lock. This restriction was protested to the Protecting Power without results because the Commandant refused to forward the correspondence to Switzerland. A visit by the Protecting Power in July gave the SAO the opportunity of bringing these facts to the representatives' attention. Even though the commandant was spoken to severely about his most recent violations of the Geneva Convention, it was not until the Protecting Power informed the German Foreign Office which in turn wrote to Oberst Scherer directly that Red Cross and personal parcels were allowed PW in the arrest-lock.

After Oberst Warnstadt became commandant conditions became even worse. Instructions to the guards on the use of firearms were liberalized, and on 18 March 1945, 2d Lieutenant E.F. Wyman was killed and a British officer was wounded during an air raid warning that was not heard by 95% of the men in the same area. The defective system and the "shoot to kill" order were responsible for this incident.

Both Oberst Warnstadt and Oberst Scherer were inclined to inflict mass punishment by restricting an entire barrack for one person's infraction of a rule, and several protests to the Protecting Power had to be made about these occurrences. However, little satisfaction was gained from these protests, and mass punishments continued to be the general policy.

Food

Food was handled through a central warehouse for Red Cross parcels with all German food being prepared in separate kitchens in each compound. The German food was prepared by personnel hired by the German authorities or by Czechs who had been captured while serving with the Allied forces. Red Cross parcels, when available, were issued at the rate of one per person per week. The distribution of this food was made by the barrack blocks, each barrack receiving one-third of its total weekly parcels three days a week. All food with the exception of the German ration was prepared by individuals in their own rooms. Only North 1 Compound used their communal kitchen to combine the German ration and the Red Cross parcel items to supply complete meals.

The German food ration up until 1 October 1944 consisted of 1200 to 1800 calories daily per man. The ration was gradually cut until it contained only 800 calories. In September, October and November 1944, Red Cross supplies became so low that they too, had to be cut. During this period men were put on half-parcels each week. A shipment was received in November and PW then drew the normal parcel each week during December in addition to a Christmas parcel. In January the parcel supply again took a drop, and the men received one-half parcel per week and in February only one-quarter parcel per week. From 3 March 1945 until the last of the month no parcels were distributed, and the German ration deteriorated to an extent that toward the end of the month, men became so weak that many would fall down when attempting to get from their beds. American "MP's" were placed around garbage cans to prevent the starving PW from eating out of the cans and becoming sick. About 1 April 1945 a shipment was received from Lubeck via Sweden, and from that time until the evacuation the men obtained sufficient food.

Until this "starvation" period, the normal daily menu would consist of about six potatoes, one-fifth of a loaf of bread, margarine, marmalade, a small piece of meat (usually horsemeat), two vegetables (cabbage, parsnips, beets or turnips) tea and coffee, and a small amount of sugar. In addition, a thin barley soup was frequently served.

Health

In January 1944 a medical record of every man in camp was established, and as new PW arrived, they were required to make out a similar record. The form consisted of recording any injuries or illnesses incurred since MIA, the nature of these, and the medical treatment needed by those not fully recovered while in camp. Illnesses and injuries incurred at camp were also included.

Originally the camp contained only a small infirmary which could accommodate thirty bed patients and provide two rooms for daily sick call. In September 1944 another large barrack was built adjoining the infirmary and provided adequate facilities for hospitalization. When the infirmary was enlarged, the Protecting Power made arrangements with the IRCC to send additional supplies which included surgical instruments. Although serious cases were sent to Stalag 2-A at Newbrandenburg, the hospital staff at the camp was able to care for most of the ill and injured men.

The most serious detriment to the health of PW at this camp was the very poor sanitation. One bathhouse containing 10 shower-heads represented the only facilities for over 4,000 officers to bathe, and it was also used as a delousing plant for new arrivals or for any outbreaks of body-crawling insects. Early in 1945 an additional bathhouse was completed which contained 20 shower-heads. Insufficient quantities of wash basins and soap made laundering difficult, and no arrangements were made to care for the men's laundry outside of the camp. Bed linen was theoretically changed once a month, but this period was greatly extended with the influx of new PW. No facilities existed for the disposal of garbage not cared for by incinerators, and latrine and wash drains were so unsatisfactory that the areas around the barracks were frequently flooded.

The climate in the region was extremely cold, and both the number of stoves and the amount of fuel issued were insufficient to maintain good health. Upper respiratory diseases were a source of concern to the medical staff, and this became a great danger when the Germans required the shutters to remain closed during the night. Small ventilators were allowed open but offered insufficient air under the crowded conditions.

The medical staff of two British doctors and six orderlies was too small, and although additional doctors were requested, it was not until 1 March 1945 that an American doctor, Captain Wilbur E. McKee arrived. The staff was considered very capable and cooperative at all times, but was hampered by the lack of medical supplies and facilities to handle such a large number of patients.

Clothing

The Germans issued no clothing to the PW at this camp except 30 sets of German coveralls and 30 pairs of wooden shoes for the kitchen help; these were obtained only after repeated protests. The Red Cross supplied quantities of uniforms and blankets, but the camp expanded so rapidly that supplies were always inadequate until the summer of 1944 when a very large shipment was received enabling each man in camp to have two complete uniforms and two blankets. However, in February 1945 many of the uniforms had become threadbare and a redistribution of uniforms was made.

The Germans also confiscated many articles of clothing under the claim that these items of American uniforms too closely resembled civilian clothes, thus violating the security regulations of the camp.

Work

All PW at the camp were either officers or non-commissioned officers, and although many of the NCO's came to the camp as volunteers for work in a "supervisory" capacity, they refused to work upon arriving at the camp and learning that the work was actually orderly duty. British and American privates were promised for these duties but never arrived.

Pay

The rate of pay was RM 7.50 for the officers. Money was turned over to the Finance Officer who in turn made available to each officer sufficient amounts to take care of postage and toilet articles. The unused portion was made a part of the communal fund for the enlisted men.

Mail

All incoming mail at Stalag Luft 1 was censored at Stalag Luft 3 until January 1945. Some pieces of mail received at the camp had been in transit six and seven months, and normally men would be in the camp seven months before receiving their first news from home. The average time in transit from the United States was 19 weeks. Toward the end of the war, the transit time was longer due to the transportation tie-up.

Great difficulty was experienced in getting letter and card forms in sufficient quantities to have the normal ration issued each month. On several occasions none was available even though the commandant was informed that stocks were low and that additional supplies should be requisitioned.

Officers were permitted to send three letters and four postcards per month, while the enlisted men were allowed to send two letters and four postcards per month.

Morale

The morale of men was particularly good after the Allied invasion of the continent, and remained high until the starvation period during which time there was a definite decline. Normally speaking, however, the morale was at all times good.

Welfare

Representatives of the International Red Cross visited the camp approximately every four months, sometimes at the same time that the representative of the Protecting Power made inspection trips. Every attempt was made by these representatives to keep ample supplies of food parcels and clothing issues flowing into the camp, and the shortages of supplies were blamed on lack of cooperation of the Commandant of the camp or the bogging down of transportation facilities. The Protecting Power representatives did not seem to bring sufficient pressure to bear on the German officials to improve the camp conditions in the earlier stages, but after the Spring of 1944 improvements would be noted after these visits. The Protecting Power delegates promptly turned over to the IRCC and the YMCA all of the requisitions for supplies and equipment. These agencies were equally prompt in filling the orders. The YMCA representative went to the camp every 3 to 4 months and arranged for supplies of athletic equipment, books, musical instruments, theatrical supplies as well as telegrams to the next of kin. His visits were considered very valuable as morale builders.

Religion

Protestant services were held from the time the camp was opened, but it was eight months before a Catholic priest was obtained for men of that faith. As the strength of the camp increased the Germans obtained additional clergymen until there were three Catholic and three Protestant chaplains. Unfortunately only two of the compounds offered satisfactory facilities for holding church services, and requests for other compounds to use the communal mess hall in North 1 compound were refused. Outdoor services were held when weather permitted.

Recreation

Outdoor recreation was hampered through lack of sufficient sportsgrounds. Only [at] West and North 1 Compounds were there full-sized football and baseball fields, and although teams from other compounds were permitted to use this field for competitive sports, spectators were excluded. Excellent sports equipment was available throughout the camp, however, and the men in the other compounds managed to improvise games suitable to the limited space.

The two bands formed at the camp offered extremely good entertainment and provided music for theatrical productions which were frequently given. A radio was received through the YMCA, but the extra loudspeakers were not permitted in barracks by the Detaining Power.

An educational program was started early in 1944. When the camp became overcrowded, and communal rooms had to be sacrificed for living quarters, group study was no longer possible. Technical books of all kinds were available in the well-stocked libraries for individual study.

Many of the men with artistic talent spent their time in creative work, such as wood-carving, painting, drawing, and constructing models. The Recreation Officer collected all of these items for a post-war exhibit since an unusual amount of talent was apparent in the results.

Liberation

On 30 April 1945 the SAO had several conferences with the Commandant, who had orders to move the camp to prevent it from falling into the hands of the Russians. The SAO stated PW would not move unless force was used, and the commandant finally agreed to avoid bloodshed. At about 2200 that evening, the guards turned out the perimeter and street lights. A few moments later these same guards were observed marching out of the camp leaving the gate unlocked. As soon as this news was conveyed to the SAO, he formally took over the camp. The following morning the PW military police of the camp were put in charge of all guard stations to see that the men remained orderly and stayed in the camp. Another organization was formed to serve as exterior guards to prevent wandering parties of Germans from coming into the camp. On 1 May 1945 contact parties were sent out to make contact with Russian advance troops. After two or three days of having Russian commanders of scouting parties visit the camp, the Russian commander of the area was finally reached, and arrangements were made to provide food for the PW.

Evacuation

Although the actual liberation was performed by the Russians, no effort was made by them to evacuate the PW from the area. On 6 May 1945, Colonel Byerly, the former SAO left camp with two officers of a British airborne division and flew to England the following day. After reporting to 8th Air Force headquarters on the conditions of the camp, arrangements were made to evacuate the liberated PW by air. This operation was completed on 15 May 1945.

STALAG LUFT 3
(Air Force Officers)

Location

Until 27 January 1945, Stalag Luft 3 was situated in the Province of Silesia, 90 miles southeast of Berlin, in a stand of fir trees south of Sagan (51° 35' North latitude - 15° 19' 30" East longitude).

In the January exodus, the South Compound and Center Compound moved to Stalag 7A, Moosburg (48° 27' North latitude - 11° 57' East longitude). The West Compound and North Compound moved to Stalag 13 D, Nurnberg-Langwasser (49° 27' North latitude - 11° 50' East longitude) and then proceeded to Moosburg, arriving 20 April 1945.

Strength

On 14 April 1942 Lt. (j.g.) John E. Dunn, 0-6545, U.S. Navy, was shot down by Germans and subsequently became the first American flyer to be confined in Stalag Luft 3, then solely a prison camp for officer PW of the Royal Air Force. By 15 June 1944, U.S. Air Force officers in camp numbered 3,242, and at the time of the evacuation in January 1945, the International Red Cross listed the American strength as 6,844. This was the largest American officers' camp in Germany.

Description

When the first Americans arrived in 1942, the camp consisted of two compounds or enclosures, one for the RAF officers and one for RAF NCOs. The rapid increase in strength forced the Germans to build four more compounds, with USAAF personnel taking over the Center, South, West and sharing the North Compound with the British. Adjoining each compound the Germans constructed other enclosures called "vorlagers" in which most of the camp business was transacted and which held such offices as supply, administration and laundry.

Each compound enclosed 15 one-story, wooden barracks or "blocks." These, in turn, were divided into 15 rooms ranging in size from 24 feet by 15 feet to 14 feet by six feet. Occupants slept in double-decker bunks and for every three or four men the Germans provided simple wooden tables, benches and stools. One room, equipped with a cooking range, served as a kitchen. Another, with six porcelain basins, was the washroom. A third, with one urinal and two commodes, was the latrine.

A "Block" could house 82 men comfortable, but with the growth in numbers of PW, rooms designed for eight men began holding 10 and then 12, and the middle of September 1944 saw new PW moving into tents outside the barracks.

Two barbed wire fences 10 feet high and five feet apart surrounded each compound. In between them lay tangled barbed wire concertinas. Paralleling the barbed wire and 25 feet inside the fence ran a "warning wire" strung on 30-inch wooden posts. The zone between the warning wire and the fence was forbidden territory, entrance to which was punishable by sudden death.

At the corners of the compound and at 50-yard intervals around its perimeter rose 40-foot wooden guard towers holding Germans armed with rifles and machine guns.

U.S. Personnel

Lt. Col. Albert P. Clark, Jr., captured on 26 July 1942, became the first Senior American Officer, a position he held until the arrival of Col. Charles G. Goodrich some two months later. The enforced seclusion of individual compounds necessitated the organization of each as an independent PW camp. At the time of the move from Sagan, camp leaders were as follows:

Senior Allied Officer	Brigadier General Arthur W. Vanaman
SAO South Compound	Col. Charles G. Goodrich
SAO Center Compound	Col. Delmar T. Spivey
SAO West Compound	Col. Darr H. Alkire
SAO North Compound	Lt. Col. Edwin A. Bland

The staff of a compound was organized into two categories:

Main Staff Depts.	*Secondary Staff Depts.*
a. Adjutant	a. Mail
b. German property	b. Medical
c. German rations	c. Coal
d. Red Cross food	d. Finance
e. Red Cross clothing	e. Canteen
f. Education & Recreation	f. Orderlies, etc.

The basic unit for organization was the barrack building or block. Block staffs were organized to include the same functions as the Compound Staff, and the blocks themselves were sub-divided into squads of 10 men each.

Each compound had a highly organized Security Committee.

German Personnel

The original commandant of Stalag Luft 3 was Oberst von Lindeiner, an old-school aristocrat with some 40 years of army service. Courteous and considerate at first sight, he was inclined to fits of uncontrolled rage. Upon one occasion he personally threatened a PW with a pistol. He was, however, more receptive to PW requests than any other commandant.

After the British mass escape of March 1944, Oberst von Lindeiner was replaced by Oberstleutnant Cordes, who had been a PW in World War I. A short while later Cordes was succeeded by Oberst Braune, direct and business-like. Stricter than his predecessors, he displayed less sympathy toward PW requests. Nevertheless, he was able to stop misunderstandings such as the one resulting in guards shooting into the compounds. In general, commandants tended to temporize when dealing with PW, or else to avoid granting their requests entirely.

Most disliked by PW were the Abwehr or Security officers - Hauptmann Breuli and his successor Major Kircher.

The Luftwaffe guards were fourth rate troops -

either peasants too old for combat duty or young men convalescing after long tours of duty or wounds received at the front. They had almost no contact with PW. In addition to uniformed sentries, soldiers in fatigues were employed by the Germans to scout the interiors of the compounds. These "ferrets" hid under barracks, listened to conversations, looked for tunnels and made themselves generally obnoxious to the PW. The German complement totaled 800.

Occasionally, as after the March 1944 mass escape, Gestapo groups descended upon the camp for a long, thorough search.

Treatment

Because of their status as officers and the fact that their guards were Luftwaffe personnel, the men at Stalag Luft 3 were accorded treatment better than that granted other PW in Germany. Generally, their captors were correct in their adherence to many of the tenets of the Geneva Convention. Friction between captor and captive was constant and inevitable, nevertheless, and the strife is well illustrated by the following example.

On 27 March 1944 the Germans instituted an extra appel (roll call) to occur any time between the regular morning and evening formations. Annoyed by an indignity which they considered unnecessary, PW fought the measure with a passive resistance. They milled about, smoked, failed to stand at attention and made it impossible for the lager officer to take a count. Soon they were dismissed. Later in the day another appel was called. This time the area was lined with German soldiers holding rifles and machine guns in readiness to fire. Discreetly, PW allowed the appel to proceed in an orderly fashion. A few days later, nevertheless, probably as a result of this deliberate protest against German policy, the unwonted extra appel was discontinued.

Since the murder of 50 RAF flyers has been attributed to the Gestapo, acts of atrocious mistreatment involving the regular Stalag Luft 3 guard complement may be narrowed down to two.

About 2200 hours, 29 December 1943, a guard fired a number of shots into one barrack without excuse or apparent purpose. One bullet passed through the window and seriously wounded the left leg of Lt. Col. John D. Stevenson. Although Col. Stevenson spent the next six months in hospitals, the wound has left him somewhat crippled.

About 1230 hours, 9 April 1944, during an air raid by American bombers, Cpl. Cline C. Miles was standing in the cookhouse doorway. He was facing the interior. Without warning a guard fired at "a man" standing in the doorway. The bullet entered the right shoulder of Cpl. Miles and came out through his mouth, killing him instantly.

Food

German rations, instead of being the equivalent of those furnished depot troops, compared with those received by non-working civilians - the lowest in Germany. While insufficient, these foods provided the bulk of staples, mainly through bread and potatoes. A PWs average daily issue of foods, with caloric content included, follows:

Type of food	Grams	Calories
Potatoes	390	331
Bread	350	910
Meat	11	20
Barley, Oats, Etc.	21	78
Kohlrabi	247	87
Dried Vegetables	14	38
Margarine	31	268
Cheese	10	27
Jam	25	69
Sugar	25	100
TOTALS	1124	1928

A conservative estimate of the caloric requirement of a person sleeping nine hours a day and taking very little exercise is 2,150 calories. German rations, therefore, fell below the minimum requirement for healthy nutrition.

Food came from four other sources: Red Cross parcels, private parcels, occasional canteen purchases and gardens. Of the Red Cross parcels, after the spring of 1943, 40% were American, 25% British, 25% Canadian and 10% miscellaneous such as New Zealand parcels, Christmas parcels and bulk issue from the British colony of Argentina. These were apportioned at the rate of one per man per week during periods of normal supply. If the International Red Cross at Geneva felt that transportation difficulties would prevent the usual delivery, it would notify the camp parcel officer to limit the issue to one-half parcel per man per week. Such a situation arose in September 1944 when all Stalag Luft 3 went on half parcels. Average contents of American and British parcels were as follows:

American Food	Weight (oz.)	British Food	Weight (oz.)
Spam	12	Meat Roll	10
Corned Beef	12	Stew	12
Salmon	8	Cheese	4
Cheese	8	Dried Fruit	6
Dried Fruit	16	Biscuits	10
Biscuits	?	Condensed Milk	14
Klim	16	Margarine	8
Margarine	16	Tea	2
Soluble	4	Sugar	4
Sugar	8	Cocoa	6
Orange Powder	4	Jam	10
Liver Paste	6	Powdered Eggs	2
Chocolate	4	Chocolate	4
		Vegetables	8

Since the kitchen equipment of 10 boilers and two ovens per compound was obviously inadequate, almost all food was prepared by the various room messes in the blocks. These messes obtained from the kitchen only hot water and, four times a week, hot soup. Cooking within the block was performed on a range whose heating surface was three square feet. During winter months, PW were able to use the heating stoves in their rooms as well. With few exceptions, each room messed by itself. All food was pooled, and room cooks were responsible for serving it in digestible and appetizing, if possible, form. Since the stove schedule provided for cooking periods from 3 p.m. to 9 p.m., some rooms ate their main meal in mid-afternoon, while others dined fashionably late. Below is a typical day's menu:

Breakfast - 9 a.m.
 Two slices of German bread with spread
 Coffee (soluble) or tea
Lunch - noon
 Soup (on alternate days)
 Slice of German bread
 Coffee or tea
Supper - 5:30 p.m.
 Potatoes
 One-third can of meat
 Vegetables (twice a week)
 Slice of German bread
 Coffee or tea
Evening snack - 10 p.m.
 Dessert (pie, cake, etc.)
 Coffee or cocoa

A unique PW establishment was *Foodacco* whose chief function was to provide PW with a means of exchange and a stable barter market where, for example, cocoa could be swapped for cigars. Profits arising from a two per cent commission charged on all transactions was credited to a communal camp fund.

Health

Despite confinement, crowding, lack of medical supplies and poor sanitary facilities, health of PW was astonishingly good.

For trivial ailments, the compounds maintained a first aid room. More serious cases were sent to one of the two sick quarters within the camp. Sick quarters for the South Compound originally consisted of a small building with 24 beds, a staff of three PW doctors and some PW orderlies. This also served the North and West Compounds. The Center Compound had its own dispensary and two PW doctors. On 1 June 1944, the three-compound sick quarters was replaced by a new building with 60 beds.

The Germans furnished very few medical supplies. As a result, PW depended almost wholly on the Red Cross. Large shipments of supplies, including much-needed sulfa drugs, began to arrive in the autumn of 1944. PW were also glad to receive a small fluoroscope and thermometers.

Most common of the minor illnesses were colds, sore throats, influenza, food poisoning and skin diseases. When a PW needed an X-ray or the attentions of a specialist, he was examined by a German doctor. It usually took months to obtain these special attentions. Cases requiring surgery were sent to one of the English hospitals, as a rule Lamsdorf or Obermassfeld. Emergency cases went to a French hospital at Stalag 8C, one mile distant.

Dental care for the North, West and South Compounds was provided by a British dentist and an American dental student. In 14 months, they gave 1,400 treatments to 308 PW from the South Compound alone.

Sanitation was poor. Although PW received a quick delousing upon entry into the camp, they were plagued by bedbugs and other parasites. Since there was no plumbing, both indoor and outdoor latrines added to the sanitation problem in summer. PW successfully fought flies by scrubbing aborts daily, constructing fly traps and screening latrines with ersatz burlap in lieu of wire mesh.

Bathing faciliates were extremely limited. In theory the German shower houses could provide each man with a three-minute hot shower weekly. In fact, however, conditions varied from compound to compound and if a PW missed the opportunity to take a hot shower he resorted to a sponge bath with water he had heated himself - the only other hot water available the year around.

Clothing

In 1943, Germany still issued booty clothing of French, Belgian or English derivation to PW. This practice soon ceased, making both Britons and Americans completely dependent on clothing received from the Red Cross. An exception to the rule was made in the winter of 1943 when the camp authorities obtained 400 old French overcoats from Anglo-American PW.

Gradually, Americans were able to replace their RAF type uniforms with GI enlisted men's uniforms, which proved extremely serviceable. When stock of clothing permitted, each PW was maintained with the following wardrobe:

1 Overcoat
1 Blouse (Jacket)
2 Shirts, Wool or Cotton
1 Pr. Wool Trousers
2 Pr. Winter Underwear
2 Pr. Socks
1 Pr. Gloves
1 Sweater
1 Pr. High Shoes
1 Belt or Suspenders
1 Cap
4 Handkerchiefs
1 Blanket (added to 2 German blankets)

Work

Officers were never required to work. To ease the situation in camp, however, they assumed many house-keeping chores such as shoe repairing, distributing food, scrubbing their own rooms and performing general repair work on barracks.

Other chores were carried out by a group of 100 American orderlies whose work was cut to a minimum and whose existence officers tried to make as comfortable as possible under the circumstances.

Pay

The monthly pay scale of officers in Germany was as follows:

F/O and 2d Lt.	72 Reichsmarks
1st Lt.	81 Reichsmarks
Capt.	96 Reichsmarks
Major	108 Reichsmarks
Lt. Col.	120 Reichsmarks
Col.	150 Reichsmarks

Americans adhered closely to the financial policy originated by the British in 1940-42. No money was handled by individual officers but was placed by the accounts officer into individual accounts of each after a sufficient deduction had been made to meet the financial needs of the camp. These deductions, not to exceed 50% of any officer's pay, took care of laundry, letter forms, airmail postage, entertainments, escape damages and funds transmitted monthly to the NCO camps, which received no pay until July 1944.

Officers at Stalag Luft 1 contributed 33% of their pay to the communal fund, and the entire policy was approved by the War Department on 14 October 1943. Since the British Government unlike the U.S.A., deducted PW pay from army pay, Americans volunteered to carry out all canteen purchases with their own funds, but to maintain joint British-American distribution just as before.

Because of the sudden evacuation from Sagan, Allied PW had no time to meet with German finance authorities and reconcile outstanding Reichsmark balances. The amount due the U.S.A. alone from the German Government totals 2,984,932.75 Reichsmarks.

Mail

Mail from home or sweetheart was the life-blood of PW. Incoming mail was normally received six days a week, without limit as to number of letters or number of sheets per letter. (German[s] objected only to V-mail forms.) Incoming letters could travel postage free, but those clipper-posted made record time. Correspondence could be carried on with private persons in any country outside of Germany; Allied, neutral or enemy. Within Germany correspondence with next-of-kin only was permitted. A PW could write one letter per month to next-of-kin in another PW camp or internees' camp.

South Compound Incoming Mail

Month	Letters	Per Capita	Age
Sep 43	3,190	3	11 weeks
Oct 43	5,392	5	10 weeks
Nov 43	9,125	9	10 weeks
Dec 43	24,076	24	8 weeks
Jan 44	7,680	7	12 weeks
Feb 44	10,765	9	12 weeks
Mar 44	11,693	10	12 weeks
Apr 44	16,355	15	12 weeks
May 44	15,162	13	13 weeks
Jun 44	13,558	11	14 weeks
Jul 44	26,440	20	14 weeks
Aug 44	14,264	11	15 weeks
Sep 44	10,277	8	16 weeks

The travel time reverted to 11-12 weeks in the autumn of 1944, with airmail letters sometimes reaching camp in four to six weeks. All mail to Luftwaffe-held PW was censored in Sagan by a staff of German civilian men and women.

Outgoing mail was limited, except for special correspondence, to three letter forms and four cards per PW per month. Officers above the rank of major drew six letters and four cards while enlisted men received two letter forms and four cards. Protected personnel received double allotments. PW paid for these correspondence forms and for airmail-postage as well.

South Compound Outgoing Mail

Month	Letters	Postage in RMs
Sep 43	3,852	924.60
Oct 43	6,711	2494.60
Nov 43	7,781	2866.66
Dec 43	7,868	2968.00
Jan 44	7,811	2915.30
Feb 44	7,968	2907.10
Mar 44	7,916	3095.80
Apr 44	8,460	3154.90
May 44	8,327	3050.20
Jun 44	10,189	3789.60
Aug 44	8,780	3,366.50
Sep 44	8,777	3288.30

Each 60 days, a PW's next-of-kin could mail him a private parcel containing clothing, food and other items not forbidden by Germans or U.S. government regulations. These parcels, too, were thoroughly examined by German censors.

Morale

Morale was exceptionally high. PW never allowed themselves to doubt an eventual Allied victory and their spirits soared at news of the European invasion. Cases of demoralization were individual, caused for the most part by reports of infidelities among wives or sweethearts, or lack of mail, or letters in which people failed completely to comprehend PW's predicament. Compound officers succeeded in keeping their charges busy either physically or mentally and in maintaining discipline. The continual arrival of new PW with news of home and the air force also helped to cheer older inmates.

Welfare

The value of the Protecting Power in enforcing the provisions of the Geneva Convention lay principally in the pressure they were able to bring to bear.

Although they might have agreed with the PW point of view, they had no means of enforcing their demands upon the Germans, who followed the Geneva Convention only insofar as its provisions coincided with their policies. But the mere existence of a Protecting Power, a third party, had its beneficial effect on German policy.

Direct interview was the only satisfactory traffic with the Protecting Power. Letters usually required six months for answer - if any answer was received. The sequence of events at a routine visit of Protecting Power representatives was as follows: Granting by the German[s] of a few concessions just prior to visit; excuses given by the Germans to the representative; conference of representative with compound seniors; conference of representative with Germans. Practical benefits usually amounted to minor concessions from the Germans.

PW of Stalag Luft 3 feel a deep debt of gratitude toward the Red Cross for supplying them with food and clothing, which they considered the two most important things in their PW camp life. Their only complaint is against the Red Cross PW bulletin for its description of Stalag Luft 3 in terms more appropriately used in depicting life on a college campus than a prison camp.

PW also praised the YMCA for providing them generously with athletic equipment, libraries, public address systems and theatrical materials. With YMCA headquarters established in Sagan, the representative paid many visits to camp.

Religion

On 1 December 1942, the Germans captured Capt. M. E. McDonald with a British Airborne Division in Africa. Because he was "out of the cloth" they did not officially recognize him as a clergyman, nevertheless, he was the accredited chaplain for the camp and conducted services for a large Protestant congregation. He received a quantity of religious literature from the YMCA and friends in Scotland.

In April 1942, Father Philip Goudres, Order of Mary Immaculate, Quebec, Canada, became the Catholic Chaplain to a group which eventually numbered more than 1,000 PW. Prayer books were received from Geneva and rosary beads from France.

On 12 September 1943, a Christian Science Group was brought together in the South Compound under the direction of 2d Lt. Rudolph K. Grumm, 0-749387. His reading material was forwarded by the Church's War Relief Committee, Geneva, as was that of 1st Lt. Robert R. Brunn active in the Center Compound.

Thirteen members of the Church of Jesus Christ of Latter Day Saints, sometimes known as the Mormon Church, held their first meeting in the South Compound on 7 November 1943. 1st Lt. William E. McKell was nominated as presiding Elder and officiated at subsequent weekly meetings. Material was supplied by the European Student Relief Fund, the Red Cross, the YMCA and the Swiss Mission of the Church.

Recreation

Reading was the greatest single activity of PW. The fiction lending library of each compound was enlarged by books received from the YMCA and next-of-kin until it totaled more than 2,000 volumes. Similarly, the compounds' reference libraries grew to include over 500 works of technical nature.

These books came from the European Student Relief Fund of the YMCA and from PW who had received them from home.

Athletics were second only to reading as the most popular diversion. Camp areas were cleared and made fit playing fields at first for cricket and rugby and later for softball, touch football, badminton, deck tennis and volleyball. In addition, PW took advantage of opportunities for pingpong, wrestling, weight lifting, horizontal and parallel bar work, hockey and swimming in the fire pool. The bulk of athletic equipment was supplied by the YMCA.

The "Luftbandsters," playing on YMCA instruments, could hold its own with any name band in the U.S.A. according to those who heard them give various performances. PW formed junior bands of less experienced players and also a glee club.

Through the services of the YMCA, PW were shown seven films, five somewhat dated Hollywood features and two German musical comedies.

Other activities included card playing, broadcasting music and news over a camp amplifier called "Station KRGY," reading the "Circuit" and "Kriegie Times" journals issued by PW thrice weekly, following world events in the PW news room, attending the Education Department's classes which ranged from Aeronautics to Law, painting, sketching and the inevitable stroll around the compound perimeter track.

Sagan Evacuation

At 2100 hours on 27 January 1945, the various compounds received German orders to move out afoot within 30 minutes. With an eye on the advancing Red Armies, PW had been preparing two weeks for such a move. Thus the order came as no surprise. In barracks bags, in knotted trousers and on makeshift sleds they packed a minimum of clothing and a maximum of food - usually one parcel per man. Each man abandoned such items as books, letters, camp records and took his overcoat and one blanket. Between 2130 and 2400 hours, all men except some 200 too weak to walk, marched out into the bitter cold and snow in a column of threes - destination unknown. Their guards, drawn from the camp complement, bore rifles and machine pistols. They marched all night, taking ten-minute breaks every hour.

The exodus was harrowing to PW of all compounds but especially those of the South, which made the 55 kilometers from Sagan to Muskau in 27 hours with only four hours sleep. Rations consisted only of bread and margarine obtained from a horse-drawn wagon. PW slept in unheated barns. At Muskau, on the verge of exhaustion, they were billeted in a blast furnace, which was warm and an empty heating plant, which was cold. Here they were given a 30-hour delay for recuperation. Even so, some 60 men incapable of marching farther had to be left behind. The 25 kilometers from Muskau to Spremberg on 31 January, the South Compound, plus 200 men from the West Compound, went to Stalag 7A at Moosburg [sic]. They traveled two days and two nights in locked, unmarked freight cars - 50 men to a car. On 7 February, the Center Compound joined them. The North Compound fell in with the West Compound at Spremberg and on 2 February entrained for Stalag 13D, Nurnberg, which they reached after a trip of two days.

Throughout the march the guards, who drew rations identical with PW's, treated their charges with sympathy and complained at the harshness they all had to undergo. German civilians encountered during the trek were generally considerate, bartering with PW and sometimes supplying them with water.

Stalag 13D Conditions

Conditions at Stalag 13D, where PW stayed for two months, were deplorable. The barracks originally built to house delegates to the Nazi party gatherings at the shrine city, had recently been inhabited by Italian PW who left them filthy. There was no room to exercise, no supplies, nothing to eat out of and practically nothing to eat inasmuch as no Red Cross food parcels were available upon the Americans' arrival. The German ration consisted of 300 grams of bread, 250 grams of potatoes, some dehydrated vegetables and a little margarine. After the first week, sugar was not to be had and soon the margarine supply was exhausted. After three weeks, and in answer to an urgent request, 4,000 Red Cross food parcels arrived from Dulag Luft, Wetzlar. Shortly thereafter,

the Swiss came to make arrangements for sending parcels in American convoy, and soon Red Cross parcels began to arrive in GI (Red Cross) trucks.

Throughout this period, large numbers of American PW were pouring into camp - 1,700 from Stalag Luft 4, 150 a day from Dulag Luft and finally some men from Oflag 64.

Sanitation was lamentable. The camp was infested with lice, fleas and bedbugs. Three thousand men, each with only two filthy German blankets, slept on the bare floors. Toilet facilities during the day were satisfactory, but the only night latrine was a can in each sleeping room. Since many men were afflicted with diarrhea, the can had an insufficient capacity and men perforce soiled the floor. Showers were available once every two weeks. Barracks were not heated. Only 200 kilograms of coal were provided for cooking. Morale dropped to its lowest ebb, but Col. Darr H. Alkire succeeded in maintaining discipline.

Nurnberg Evacuation

At 1700 hours on 3 April 1945, the Americans received notice that they were to evacuate the Nurnberg camp and march to Stalag 7A, Moosburg. At this point, the PW took over the organization of the march. They submitted to the German commander plans stipulating that in return for preserving order they were to have full control of the column and to march no more than 20 kilometers a day. The Germans accepted. On 4 April, with each PW in possession of a food parcel, 10,000 Allied PW began the march. While the column was passing a freight marshalling yard near the highway, some P-47s dive-bombed the yard. Two Americans and one Briton were killed and three men seriously wounded. On the following day the column laid out a large replica of an American Air Corps insignia on the road with an arrow pointing in the direction of their march. Thereafter, the column was never strafed. It proceeded to Neumarkt, to Bersheim where 4,500 Red Cross parcels were delivered by truck, then to Mulhauser where more parcels were delivered. On 9 April, the compound column reached the Danube which Col. Alkire flatly refused to cross since it meant exceeding the 20 kilometer-a-day limit. With his refusal the Germans completely lost control of the march and PW began to drop out of the column almost at will. The guards, intimidated by the rapid advance of the American Army, made no serious attempt to stop the disintegration. The main body of the column reached Stalag 7A on 20 April 1945 (See "Influx," Stalag 7A, page 196).

STALAG 7A
(Ground Force Enlisted Men
Air Force Officer Evacuees)

Location

Stalag 7A was in Bavaria 35 kilometers northeast of Munich and one kilometer north of Moosburg (48° 27' North Latitude, 11° 57' East Longitude.

Strength

This installation served several purposes: It was the camp for NCO's of the U.S. Air Force until 13 October 1943 when all 1900 were transferred to Stalag 17B. It was the transit camp from which officers and men of the ground forces captured in Africa and Italy were routed to permanent camps. It was headquarters for working parties of ground force privates who numbered 270 in September 1943, dropped to nil the following month and rose to 1100 in July 1944. As Germany collapsed in the spring of 1945, it became the final gathering place for no fewer than 7948 officers and 6944 enlisted men moved from other PW camps.

Description

Situated in a flat area surrounded by hills, the camp was roughly a square divided into three main compounds which in turn were subdivided into small stockades. The *Nordlager* held newly arrived PW two days while they were searched, medically examined and deloused. The *Suedlager* held only Russians. The *Hauptlager* housed PW of other nationalities - French, Polish, Jugoslav (Serb), British and American. Although nationalities were segregated by compounds, intercommunication existed. No effort was made to keep transient American PW from the permanent inmates. Seven guard towers and the usual double barbed wire fence formed the camps perimeter.

Barracks were rectangular wooden buildings divided into two sections, A and B, by a central room used for washing and eating. In it were a water faucet and water pump and some tables. The barracks chief and assistant had a small corner room to themselves. PW slept on triple-deck wooden bunks and gunny-sack mattresses filled with excelsior. Gradually the number of men per barracks increased from 180 to 400. Men slept on tables, floors and the ground.

U.S. Personnel

Because of the camp's shifting population, leaders were changed frequently. Among them were:

MOC Cpl. Charles Daramus	February 1943
MOC S/Sgt. Earl Benson	March 1943
MOC S/Sgt. Clyde M. Bennett	March 1943
MOC S/Sgt. Kenneth J. Kurtenbach	July-Oct 1943
MOC M/Sgt. John M. McMahan	June-Sept 1943
MOC S/Sgt. James P. Caparel	Oct 1943 - Feb 1944
MOC T/Sgt. Philip M. Beeman	Feb 1944 - Apr 1945
SAO Col. A.Y. Smith (AAF)	Feb - Mar 1945
SAO Col. Paul R. Goode	April 1945
Chaplain 1st Lt. Eugene L. Daniel	Feb 1944 - Apr 45

Major Fred H. Beaumont, Medical Corps
Captain Gordan Keppel, Medical Corps
Captain Louis Salerno, Medical Corps
1st Lt. James Godfrey, Medical Corps
Captain Garrold H. Nungester, Medical Corps

German Personnel

The guard was drawn from the Fourth Company of the 512th Landeschuetzen Battalion. Four officers and 200 men were employed on general duties. Ten sonderfuehrers with the rank of officers acted as interpreters. Twenty civilian men and 20 civilian women were employed as clerks in the camp. This complement was increased in April 1945 with the arrival of the entire camp staff and guard personnel of Stalag Luft 3, Nurnberg. Control of the camp, however, remained in the hands of the regular Stalag 7A staff:

Commandant	Oberst Burger
Asst. Commandant	Oberstleutnant Wohler
Security officer	Hauptman Baumler
Doctor	Oberfeldarzt Dr. Zeitzler
Lager officer	Hauptman Malheuim
Parcel officer	Sonderfuehrer Kluge

It has been reported by some PW that Burger, Malheuim and Kluge, a fanatic of the worst sort, were shot three days after the camp's liberation.

Treatment

German treatment was barely correct. In addition to harsh living conditions caused by extreme overcrowding, instances of mistreatment occasionally cropped up. Thus, at one time the Germans tried to segregate all Jews among U.S. PW, calling them in from work detachments and allotting them a separate barrack. The MOC lodged a protest with the Protecting Power immediately. When questioned, camp authorities stated that the action was taken for the Jews' own protection against possible civilian acts of violence. Eventually, the attempt at segregation failed and Jews were not distinguished from other American PW.

At the Munich kommando, guards jabbed PW with bayonets and hit them with rifle butts. In the base camp an NCO reported being kicked, then being mistaken for a Frenchman and choked during an argument and later handcuffed after an escape attempt. Once an American, using a hole in the fence instead of the open gate to go from one compound to another, was shot at but not hit. In April 1943 a Russian was shot on the compound wire and left hanging there wounded. An Englishman went to lift him off the wire and was shot but recovered. The Russian died.

In July 1943, 500 Americans without overcoats were forced to stand in formation for five hours in a heavy rain. The reasons [sic], said the Germans, was that the Americans had not been falling out at exactly 0800. During the first two weeks of August, the camp discipline officer had the PW fall out for roll call at 2100, 2400 and 0300. They were punished thus because many Americans had been escaping. PW showed no annoyance and displayed such good morale that the Germans discontinued the practice, especially since both sides knew that the PW could sleep all day but the guards could not.

Sonderfuehrer Kluge once marched 1100 PW for a whole day without food through Nurnberg so they could see the devastation wrought by Allied bombing.

In September 1943 when PW ventured out of the barracks to watch the bombing of Munich, Germans came into the compound with dogs, one of which jumped into a window and was stabbed by a retreating American. During the Regensburg raid when PW were again outside their barracks contrary to orders, a German night fighter flying over the camp reported that someone in the American compound was signaling with a mirror. After that PW were notified that anyone outside the barracks during an air raid would be shot. One night a JU 88 with lights on made two runs over the camp and dropped cement blocks. Germans then started propagandizing to the effect that the Allies were bombing their own PW camps.

Food

Here too PW depended on Red Cross food for sustenance and nourishment. Until September 1944, each PW drew his full parcel per week, and a two months' reserve was kept on hand in camp. Then the ration was cut to half a parcel per man per week and the reserve not allowed to exceed one month's sup-

ply. With the influx of PW in the beginning of 1945, stocks fell to an all time low. PW feared a complete collapse in the delivery of Red Cross food. Fortunately, this fear never materialized.

In July 1943, the MOC persuaded the Germans to issue each man a spoon and crockery plate. Cooking utensils were improvised from whatever materials could be found. Fifteen or 20 men formed mess groups, pooled their Red Cross rations and took turns in preparing them. They cooked over the small barrack's stove. Each barrack had two men on the chow detail, and the space around each stove was therefore quite crowded. At 0630 the detail brought hot water from the compound kitchen. Breakfast usually consisted of coffee and a few biscuits only. At 1130 they brought the German dinner ration - usually potatoes boiled in their jackets - from the kitchen. Sometimes spinach-type greens or barley soup were added. Five men divided one loaf of coarse German-issue bread. For supper at 1700, PW drew more potatoes. On Sundays they received greens with morsels of meat. Twice a week they had a small piece of margarine. At first, French cooks prepared the food in the compound kitchen, but since Americans thought some of the victuals disappeared in the process, they later installed their own cooks.

Health

Health was good. Several American doctors, captured early in the African and Italian campaigns accompanied PW to Stalag 7A and were able to remain with them until their transfer to permanent camps. The camp also had some British doctors and some French. Men reported to the dispensary and if deemed ill enough for hospitalization were kept in the compound infirmary which could accommodate 120 patients in 10 rooms. More serious cases went to the German camp lazaret outside the compound. This installation consisted of eight barrack-type buildings, two of which were equipped for surgical operations.

Allied doctors complained of a serious shortage of medical supplies. At first they used German drugs and such equipment as they could get. Later the Red Cross sent supplies which alleviated the shortage but did not satisfy the doctors' demands.

Despite delousings, lice and fleas troubled PW a great deal. Americans, however, unlike the Russians, never contracted typhus. For a time they suffered from skin diseases brought about by uncleanliness; washing facilities were completely unsatisfactory and a man was extremely lucky to take a shower every 15 days.

Latrines were always a source of contention

between PW and camp authorities. Complaint was constantly made that the pits were emptied only when they threatened to overflow and that there was no chloride of lime to neutralize the odor which permeated the surrounding area.

Emergency dental treatment could be obtained in the German lazaret.

Clothing

Since the Germans issued practically no clothing and the flow of needy transients through camp was heavy, the clothing shortage was always acute. From February 1943 on, the reports of the Protecting Power repeatedly carried such paragraphs as the following: The general condition of clothing is very bad. The American Red Cross should send out clothing in sufficient quantities as the cold season is approaching. Great coats and whole uniforms are badly wanted. The supply of uniforms issued by the Detaining Power is mainly old French or British uniforms in a state of mending which leaves no hope for long wear.

Clothing from the Red Cross did arrive, but not in sufficient quantity to provide for equipping newly captured PW who were wearing only the clothes in which they were captured and sometimes not even those. It was observed by a Man of Confidence that four warehouses in camp contained many new English overcoats and battle-dress outfits as well as many articles of American clothing taken from PW as they entered the camp or left it. These included aviators' leather jackets, American coveralls, combat jackets, pants, shoes, hats and shirts. It was believed by the Man of Confidence that the clothing in storage was more than enough to alleviate the suffering of both American and British PW, yet all pleas and efforts to have the Germans ameliorate the situation were to no avail.

Work

The original group of air force PW - comprised almost exclusively of NCO's - was not ordered to work, nevertheless, before going to Stalag 17B many volunteered for kommando duty merely to get on the other side of the compound's barbed wire and have more liberty. On the other hand, Germans insisted that ground force privates be assigned to labor details. Camp authorities tried to have PW volunteer for duties - a practice which the MOC advised against except in the case of farm work, which was less unpleasant than other kommando duty.

Attached to the camp were as many as 83 work detachments ranging in size from four men (usually sent out to farms) to 900 men. The three main kom-

mandos were situated in Munich, Augsburg and Landshutt. After the heavy bombing of Munich on October 4, 1944, a work detachment of some 1400 PW was formed. This party consisted of 60% Americans and 40% British. It left the Stalag at 0500 and returned at 2000. PW traveled in cattle cars from Moosburg station, standing up all the way to Munich and back. The time spent in the train going to and returning from work was three and one-half hours. During their eight working hours a day, PW cleared debris, filled bomb craters and dismantled damaged rails. Men received two meals at Munich and their regular ration at the camp. In the event of air attacks, adequate shelter was provided. There were instances of Germans pricking with bayonets and hitting them with rifle butts to make them work faster and harder.

A model farm kommando was described as follows: Twenty PW live in a farmhouse of five rooms, including a room with a stove for the cooking of Red Cross food. They sleep in three of the rooms in double-tier beds with straw mattresses and eiderdowns. Bathing and toilet facilities are primitive but similar to those used by their employer. The men sometimes eat with the farmer for whom they work and their diet, supplemented with Red Cross food, is good. Medical supplies for minor injuries are on hand and a civilian doctor takes sick parade twice a week. PW each possess two work uniforms, a dress uniform and two pair of shoes. Fourteen of the men are free on Sundays; the others do the essential farmwork, namely feeding cattle and cleaning stables. Razor blades, beer and matches are available. PW have neither time nor facilities for sports. The mail situation is satisfactory except for the pilfering of parcels en route from the stalag to the detachment.

On only three occasions was the Man of Confidence permitted to visit kommando camps for inspection. Although he turned in complaints, no improvement in conditions resulted.

Pay

In March 1943, it was reported that the matter of paying officers had not yet been settled between PW and camp authorities. In the same month, an American enlisted man on kommando was paid the equivalent of $13.00 a month. Another worker revealed that the wage rate was .70 Reichmarks a day. In July this was increased to .90 Reichmarks a day.

In April 1944, an advance of 50 Reichmarks was made to officer PW of the Allies, but in April 1945, the Senior British officer stated that officers were not being paid and that they had not received any pay statements for seven months. Similarly, the 1400 man kommando working daily in the debris of Munich was not paid because the labor performed by them was considered by the Germans to be "emergency" labor to which anyone resident in the Reich was subject without pay.

In October 1944 it was announced that PW pay, which up to that time had been in camp money or "lager-geld" would henceforth be in Reichmarks.

Mail

During their stay at camp, transient PW were allowed to send one postcard, usually their first, in which they informed next-of-kin of their German PW number and address. PW permanently at 7A drew two postcards and two letter forms per month. Incoming mail, censored at camp, was unlimited in quantity but sporadic in arrival, especially at kommandos, which received no incoming mail for months at a time. Both outgoing and incoming letters took four months in transit, as did personal parcels. The flow of such parcels was light.

On 10 November 1944, four French PW were employed to unload coal into a bunker of the German barracks situated in the vicinity of the camp. They found that a large number of both official and private letters and cards were scattered in the coal. They picked up several loose letters as well as bunches tied together in small packages. Part of the latter included official letters addressed to the spokesmen of the different nationalities represented in the camp, coming from the Red Cross, the YMCA and other organizations. The next morning the French, British and American spokesmen went to the Commandant's office to protest and demand explanations as well as the restitution of the mail after inspection of the bunker in question. The following day, the camp commandant made it known that he would take charge of the affair personally. After a hasty censorship, a considerable number of letters (two sacks weighing 88 pounds apiece) were delivered to PW. These letters dated from the months of May, June and July 1944. It was impossible to say how long they had been in the coal. The commandant stated that an error had been made and that punishment would be inflicted, but that no letter had been burned.

The assistant American MOC was under the impression that mail - including outgoing letters - definitely had been burned. This impression was strengthened after the incident when the Germans issued additional new letter forms.

Morale

Initially morale was high. Air force NCO's repeatedly made breaks from camp, and before their trans-

fer to Stalag 17B showed their hostility toward the Germans by often refusing to salute, by failing to come to attention when a German officer entered the barracks and by their careless, slouching hands-in-pocket walk.

After their sojourn in camps in Italy, ground force PW captured in 1942-43 were pleasantly surprised by the treatment accorded them in Stalag 7A which had been a model camp for several years.

In spite of a succession of able camp leaders, morale slumped when the camp grew so crowded that PW had neither decent living quarters, nor satisfactory sanitary facilities nor sufficient clothing. Early in 1944 the MOC reported that stealing among PW was common and that fights were inevitable. However, except for a period of three weeks in December 1944, the strongest morale factor - food - was available. In the spring of 1945, although the camp was more crowded than ever, morale did not slump. Red Cross food kept coming through, and the arrival of officers with strong, experienced SAO's did much to prevent the spirit of PW from disintergrating [sic].

Welfare

A representative of the Protecting Power made a routine visit to the camp every six months. In addition he would make a special trip whenever summoned. MOC's were permitted to talk to him privately, but despite oral and written protests about both general and specific affairs of the camp, very little improvement was ever effected. The representatives repeatedly said that his hands were tied and there was nothing he could do about it. One MOC felt that the representatives were characterized by indifference and inertia until the arrival of American officers in the camp. Subsequently, their attitude changed for the better.

PW were indebted to the Red Cross for almost all their food, clothing and medical supplies. While food parcels arrived regularly and in sufficient quantity most of the time, the camp suffered a constant clothing shortage since the stocks shipped from Geneva were not enough to equip the many thousands of transient PW who passed through the camp every few months.

The first groups of PW arriving in camp reported the presence of recreational and athletic equipment which had come from the YMCA. Later, however, as the stalag evolved into a transit camp and work camp, need for such equipment was less evident and little was received.

Religion

In 1943-44, camp chaplain was 1st Lt. Eugene L. Daniel who won the admiration of both Americans and British. He had complete liberty to look after PW in the stalag, and once a month went to visit the two work detachments near Munich. He also received permission to visit the Wehrkreis PW hospital. In addition to Chaplain Daniel, Captain Arkell of the Church of England held services for Protestants.

Roman Catholics were permitted to attend weekly masses celebrated by French priests.

Jews were for a time segregated in separate barracks. Otherwise they were not discriminated against. Nor were they offered any religious services.

Conditions on kommandos varied. A few were visited by PW chaplains or attended local services, but most had no opportunity for religious observances.

Recreation

Before their transfer to 17A, the air force NCO's main diversions were baseball and bridge. They also played a good deal of volley ball. For a time they had a basketball court, but tore down the backboards for fuel. They also played horseshoes. A camp baseball league had many games between the "POWs", "Wildcats", "Bomber Aces", "Luftgangsters", and so on. At first they were allowed to use the soccer field behind their compound, a privilege later denied them. PW lacked sufficient space for recreation, especially toward the end when the compound was so completely overcrowded that Italians were sleeping in tents on the baseball diamond.

The original study program included classes in Spanish, German, French, auto mechanics, economics, bookkeeping, accounting, and mathematics. The YMCA furnished the books for these courses.

A theater kept its 1943 participants interested and its audience amused. Plays were given in a room between two barracks, and because of the limited accommodations, a show could have quite an extended run. The program was well arranged to provide continued and varied entertainment. One of the plays was "Our Town". Another was one written by the director of the group and called, "Uncle Sam Wants You". The German censor cut some of the jokes from this piece, but he did not understand most of them. The camp commandant attended one performance. There were also a minstrel show and some singing performances. When the camp became so crowded during the fall of 1943, a group of men used to go from barracks to barracks to sing each night. The band was short of instruments.

In 1944 and 1945, conditions deteriorated.

Ground force enlisted men indulged in little or no sports or recreation either because there was too little equipment for the transients or because as regular members of kommandos they were too tired after the day's work to play.

Influx

On 2 February 2000 officers of the South Compound, Stalag Luft 3, reached Stalag 7A, followed on 7 February by 2000 more from the Center Compound. They were placed in the Nordlager from which small groups were taken to be searched, deloused and sent to the main camp. No facilities were provided for washing, sanitation, cooking and only straw spread over the floors of the barracks served as bedding. In somewhat less than a week, all personnel had moved to the main camp, where conditions were little better.

Over 300 men were housed in barracks normally holding fewer than 200 men. In order to provide bunks for this number in each building, the Germans arranged three-decker in groups of four, thus accommodating 12 PW per unit. The barracks had no heat and as a result were damp, cold and unhealthful. The German administration was unprepared for the influx of new personnel and seemed completely disorganized. German rations were unbelievably poor; no inside sanitary facilities existed and there was no hot water. The 2000 PW of the Center Compound were quartered in two adjacent but separate stockades some distance from the enclosure holding their mates from the South Compound. At the rear of the barracks in each of the two stockades, a small open area - barely large enough to hold the various units for counting - was available for exercise. Aside from this, no facilities were provided for physical training or athletics. Nor was there any recreational material other than books in a traveling library provided by the YMCA.

In March the Germans provided boilers and fuel enough to allow each man to draw a pint of hot water twice daily. In order to improve the quantity and quality of German rations issued to Americans, Colonel Archibald Y. Smith, SAO, made a continuous effort to place an American officer and several enlisted men in the German kitchen. This was finally accomplished 24 March and henceforward rations improved steadily. The German administration also consented to allow groups of 50 men under guard to gather small quantities of firewood in the area adjacent to the camp. These improvements, although falling far short of the provisions of the Geneva Convention, helped a great deal to improve the mental and physical state of all the PW. During all of this period Red Cross food, initially on a half-parcel basis, was increased to full parcels and the health of the PW remained remarkably good. By this time, too, news of the Allied advances acted as a tonic on the men.

The first of April saw many PW from other camps throughout Germany evacuated to the vicinity of Stalag 7A to prevent their recapture by Allied forces pressing toward the center of the Reich. This influx brought about a state of unbelievable overcrowding and confusion. Members of the former South Compound were moved en masse into the enclosure occupied by the Center Compound. Thus 4000 PW lived in an area which had been unable to support 2000 satisfactorily. Large tents were erected in whatever space was available; straw was provided as bedding. It was not uncommon to see men sleeping on blankets in foxholes. Col. Paul R. Goode became SAO upon the arrival of officers from Oflag 64 in mid-April. Air force officers from Nurnberg arrived on 19 April. During the last 10 days of April it was felt that all PW would be left in camps, following the agreement between the German Government and the Allies, and preparations were made accordingly. However, fear that the Germans would move PW to the Salzburg redoubt and there hold them as hostages was never absent.

Liberation

On 27 April two representatives of the Protecting Power arrived at Moosburg to attend and facilitate the transfer of the PW camp from German to American authority. On the 28th it was learned from Oberst Burger, the commandant, that order was to be assured by assigning PW officers to various PW groups. Moreover, Col. Burger kept the entire German administrative staff in camp, as well as the complete guard staff. Col. Burger had not yet received from the German military authorities a reply to his question concerning the avoidance of fighting in the vicinity of the camp. The commandant asked the two Swiss to act as intermediaries between himself and the Men of Confidence.

After a conference with the Men of Confidence, the two Swiss were recalled to the commandant. It appeared that the unexpectedly rapid advance of the American forces in the region necessitated an immediate conference between the camp authorities, represented by Oberst Braune, and the local German Army Corps Commandant in order to propose the exclusion of fighting from the Moosburg region. The proposal, made by Oberst Braune and the Swiss representative, was accepted in view of Article 7 of the Geneva Convention. Appropriate instructions were given to the commander of the division in the sector in question, and the proposal was formulated for pre-sentation to the advancing Americans. According to this proposal, an area of a few kilometers around Moosburg would have to be declared a neutral zone.

At dawn on the 29th, the American and British Men of Confidence, the Swiss representative and an officer from the SS fighting division in the region drove in a white Red Cross car to the American lines. They were stopped by two tanks commanded by a colonel who drove them to the commanding general. After a long discussion with the German spokesman, the general declared the proposal unfavorable and unacceptable. The German returned to his divisional headquarters and the Swiss then drove to camp with the Men of Confidence.

At 1000, immediately after their arrival, the battle started. The ensuing fight lasted some two and a half hours, during which a shell hit one of the camp barracks injuring 12 of the guards and killing one. PW remained calm although tank shots, machine guns and small arms fire could be heard. Half an hour after the fighting abated, Combat Team A of the 14th Armored Division appeared at the camp entrance. The guards, unresisting, were disarmed. PW burst out rejoicing but did not try to leave camp. The supervision of the camp automatically went to the Men of Confidence, and an official transfer did not take place.

By instruction of the American military commander, part of the German administrative personnel remained at their posts. The remainder, including the guards, were taken as PW. The Swiss reported that treatment of German camp authorities and guards by American troops was correct.

STALAG 17B
(Air Force Non-Commissioned Officers)

Location

Stalag 17B was situated 100 meters northwest of Gneixendorf, a village which is six kilometers northwest of Krems, Austria (48° 27' N - 15° 39' E). The surrounding area was populated mostly by peasants who raised cattle and did truck farming. The camp itself was in use as a concentration camp from 1938 until 1940 when it began receiving French and Poles as the first PW.

Strength

On 13 October 1943, 1350 non-commissioned officers of the air forces were transferred from Stalag 7A to Stalag 17B, which already contained PW from France, Italy, Russia, Yugoslavia and various smaller nations. At the time of the first Protecting Power visit on 12 January 1944, the strength had increased to 2667. From then until the last days of the war a constant stream of non-commissioned officers arrived from Dulag Luft and strength reached 4237 in spite of protestations to the Detaining Power about the over-crowded conditions.

The entire camp contained 29,794 prisoners of war of various nationalities.

Description

The Americans occupied five compounds, each of which measured 175 yards by 75 yards and contained four double barracks 100 by 240 feet. The barracks were built to accommodate approximately 240 men, but at least 400 men were crowded into them after the first three months of occupancy. Each double barrack contained a washroom of six basins in the center of the building. The beds in the barracks were triple-decked, and each tier had four compartments with one man to a compartment, making a total of 12 men in each group. Each single barrack had a stove to supply heat and cooking facilities for approximately 200 men. The fuel ration for a week was 54 pounds of coal. Because of the lack of heating and an insufficient number of blankets, the men slept two to a bunk for added warmth. Lighting facilities were very poor, and many light bulbs were missing at all times.

Aside from the nine double barracks used for housing purposes, one barrack was reserved for the infirmary and the medical personnel's quarters. Half of a barrack was the library, another half for the MOC and his staff, a half for the theater, a half for Red Cross food distribution and a half for the meeting room. In addition, one barrack was used as a repair shop for shoes and clothing. Four additional barracks were added in early 1944, but two others were torn down because they were considered by the Germans to be too close to the fence, thus making it possible for PW to build tunnels for escape purposes. One of these buildings had been used as a gymnasium, and the other as a chapel. Latrines were open pit-type and were situated away from the barracks.

Two separate wire fences charged with electricity surrounded the area, and four watchtowers equipped with machine guns were placed at strategic points. At night street lights were used in addition to the searchlights from the guard towers to illuminate the area.

U.S. Personnel

Staff Sergeant Kenneth J. Kurtenbach was MOC from the opening of the camp until its evacuation. Major Fred H. Beaumont was the SAO and the med-

ical officer, but took no active part in the camp organization. Captain Stephen W. Kane was the only chaplain and acted in an advisory capacity whenever called upon. There also existed a security committee. Sgt. Kurtenbach carried on the administration with the following organization:

S/Sgt. Charles M. Belmer	Adjutant
T/Sgt. Alexander M. Haddon	School Director
S/Sgt. David H. Woo	Mail Supervisor
S/Sgt. Gerald H. Tucker	Mail Supervisor
S/Sgt. Samuel E. Underwood	Theater Supervisor
S/Sgt. Edward W. Weisenberg	Sports Supervisor

The medical staff consisted of:

Major Fred H. Beaumont
Captain Garrold H. Nungester
Captain Thomas E. Corcoran
Captain Paul G. Jacobs

German Personnel

The German personnel changed somewhat during the camp's existence, but for most of the time, the following men were in control in the positions indicated:

Oberst Kuhn	Commandant
Major Wenglorz	Security Officer
Major Eigl (Luftwaffe)	Lager Officer
Oberstabsarzt Dr. Pilger	Doctor

The blame for the bad conditions which existed at this camp has been placed on Oberst Kuhn who was both unreasonable and uncooperative. Four months elapsed after the opening of the compound before the MOC was granted an interview with the commandant to register protests, and weeks would pass before written requests were acknowledged. Frequently, orders would be issued to the MOC verbally and would never be confirmed in writing. Some cooperation was obtained from Major Eigl, but since there was friction between him (Luftwaffe) and the other German officers (Wehrmacht), his authority was extremely limited.

Treatment

The treatment at Stalag 17B was never considered good, and was at times even brutal. An example of extreme brutality occurred in early 1944. Two men attempting to escape were discovered in an out-of-bounds area adjoining the compound. As soon as they were discovered, they threw up their hands indicating their surrender. They were shot while their hands were thus upraised. One of the men died immediately, but the other was only injured in the leg. After he fell a guard ran to within 20 feet of him and fired again. The guards then turned toward the barracks and fired wild shots in that direction. One shot entered a barrack and seriously wounded an American who was lying in his bunk. Permission was denied the Americans by the Germans to bring the body of the dead man into the compound for burial, and medical treatment for the injured man in the outer zone was delayed several hours.

One PW was mentally sick when he was taken to the hospital where no provisions were made to handle cases of this type. In a moment of insanity the PW jumped from a window and ran to the fence, followed by a French doctor and orderlies who shouted to the guard not to shoot him. He was dressed in hospital pajamas which should have indicated to the guard that he was mentally unbalanced even if the doctor had not called the warning. As the patient climbed over the fence the guard shot him in the heart.

There were about 30 recorded cases of guards striking PW with bayonets, pistols and rifle butts. Protests to the commandant were always useless. In fact, on one occasion the commandant is reported to have stated that men were lucky to get off so lightly.

On another occasion an order was issued that all PW take everything that they wanted to keep and stand on the parade ground as if they were leaving camp. Nothing was touched in the barracks during the search that ensued. The same procedure was followed on the next day, and still nothing was touched. The third day, most of the PW left behind many articles of food, clothing and comfort equipment. On this occasion, German troops entered the compound with wagons and took away any and all articles left in the barracks during the parade. The Protecting Power described this act as plunder to the German commandant who finally promised to return the items, but this proved to be an almost impossible task.

Food

The normal ration to a PW for one week was as follows:

Bread:	2425 grams
Fat:	218 grams
	(68 grams were cooking fat. The remainder for spread.)
Potatoes:	(Vary up to 2800 grams. For the decrease in potatoes another leguminous plant was substituted.)
Beets or raisins:	1750 grams
Starch foods:	150 grams
Cottage cheese:	94 grams
Sugar:	175 grams
Marmalade:	175 grams
Ersatz coffee:	12 grams
Vegetables:	450 grams
Salt:	(approx.) 140 grams
Raisins:	120 grams
Dried Vegetables:	43 grams

An average daily menu would contain the following:

3 potatoes	1/2 cup of ersatz coffee
1 cup of soup	3 grams of margarine
22 grams of bread	

Vegetables were issued only when available and within the limits of the quantities available to German civilians.

When reserve supplies of Red Cross parcels were received in the camp, the German authorities reduced their issue ration. Even though protests were made to the commandant by the MOC and the Protecting Power, this practice continued. As soon as the Red Cross supplies would be exhausted, the normal ration would again be issued.

For the first three months absolutely no eating utensils were supplied. At the end of that time, one bowl and one spoon were given to each third man. PW were able to make bowls and spoons from Klim cans, which also served as drinking mugs.

On 17 October 1944, some one broke into the kitchen and stole 275 packages of cigarettes and 35 standard Red Cross parcels complete. Since the keys to the kitchen were held by the Germans it was obvious that they were responsible for the theft. However the commandant did not satisfy the MOC with his report of the investigation.

Toward the last of September 1944, the MOC received a telegram from the International Red Cross that three carloads of food, clothing and comfort supplies would arrive in a few days. These cars did in fact arrive the first of October, but the commandant neither notified the MOC nor had the cars unloaded. Instead, the cars were rerouted to another city where the contents were stored in a military park. Representatives of the IRC arrived a few days later and informed the MOC that the commandant had orders to reroute the shipment for "military reasons." Upon inspection of the cars in the nearby town, only a few of the cases proved to have been pilfered. Although there were only 3000 parcels on hand in the camp, the delivery of these cars was delayed two weeks. On 9 December two more carloads arrived and the shipment was 13 cases short. On 13 December four more cars arrived, of which one car was sixteen cases short, nine other cases pillaged, and one car with two cases missing. Seals on all four cars were broken.

Except for these incidents, the Red Cross supplies arrived in good condition.

Health

In general, health of the PW was good. They maintained their weight until the last month or so before the evacuation; they were active in games and sports, and stayed mentally healthy by keeping busy. Approximately 150 attended sick call each day with skin diseases, upper-respiratory infections and stomach ailments. About 30% of all cases at sick call were for skin diseases attributed to the conditions under which they lived. The acute shortage of water (available four hours each day), lack of hot water, lack of laundry facilities, and over-crowded sleeping conditions created many health problems, but improvements were always noticed during the summer months when the men could be outdoors a great deal of the time.

The average daily strength of the revier was 70, while the adjoining lagerlazaret cared for approximately 40, who were victims of the more serious cases of shrapnel, flak and gun wounds. Conditions there were very satisfactory in equipment, medical, clinical and surgical attendance. X-ray and consultation services were available, and were supervised by very competent medical officers who were prisoners of war of nationalities other than American.

The revier originally consisted of two ordinary barracks and two sectional "knock-down" temporary buildings. These also housed the medical personnel as previously stated. The construction was not weather tight and heating in cold weather was impossible. During most of the cold weather the water pipes froze, but the installation of a new stove in one of the buildings enabled the hospital staff to furnish an invalid diet to each patient and sufficient hot water for a bath on admission and discharge as well as once a week during his stay. The fuel supply was inadequate for these standards, but supplementary fuel was supplied by men who volunteered for wood forage details.

The two temporary buildings were set aside for isolation wards of infectious patients, but because of their poor condition, they were used only in cases of dire need.

The management of the revier was solely in the hands of the American medical PW without any interference from German authorities. A German medical officer was assigned to supervise the revier, but his daily visits concerned administrative problems only.

Clothing

The clothing condition in the camp was not unsatisfactory in the beginning because most of the men had received adequate issues when they passed through Dulag Luft. However, after the confiscation referred to in the paragraph on "Treatment," shortages became acute.

There were never sufficient blankets. The two thin cotton blankets issued by the Germans were described as "tablecloths" by many repatriates, and although the Red Cross furnished many American GI blankets, the strength increased so rapidly that only two-thirds of the men were fortunate enough to be issued one.

As in other camps, the leather flying jackets which most of the men wore at the time of their capture were taken away, but after repeated protests, some of these were returned. Shoes were a problem in the early stages, but the repair shop operated by PW alleviated the condition to some extent. The Serbian shoes issued when GI shoes were not available from the stock Red Cross supplies proved to be inadequate in quality to withstand the cold and mud.

Work

Since all of the men at this camp were non-commissioned officers, they were not required to work.

Pay

The monthly rate of pay for the PW was RM 7.50, or approximately $1.63. However, the men received this money in cash only on a few occasions. The Germans stated that the pay was to reimburse the German government for the razor blades, soap, matches, pencils, paper, etc., which were sometimes available in the canteen.

Mail

The number of mail forms issued to each prisoner varied at different times from two mail forms and two postcards to four mail forms and three postcards. There was no record of mail forms being withheld for disciplinary reasons, and apparently no check was made on the number of communications written by each PW. However, on one occasion, forms were not issued, reportedly because the printer had been bombed out. Two weeks later, a Protecting Power visit was announced and 10,000 forms were issued immediately.

Incoming mail was very irregular and considered

unsatisfactory by the PW. Since all of their mail had to be processed through Stalag Luft 3, censorship often delayed it four and five weeks. Surface letters required an average of four months for delivery as against three months for air mail. Surprisingly enough, personal parcels often arrived in two months, but the average time in transit was three to five months. In August 1944, no parcels arrived in the camp, but the following month 685 were received.

When parcels were delivered to the camp, a list of the recipients was posted in the barracks. These men were required to line up outside the delivery room. Before the PW could take possession of his parcel, the German guard would open the parcel, take everything out, and punch holes in any tinned foods. PW were permitted to keep the containers however. No items were ever confiscated from these parcels as far as could be ascertained.

Morale

The morale of PW at this camp was good as a result of two factors: the successes of the Allied armies in the field, and the recreational and educational opportunities within the camp. There was no serious trouble among the PW, and the unimportant fights and disputes which occasionally occurred seemed to spring from a desire to break the monotony. These incidents were quickly over and forgotten.

The leadership of the MOC and his staff is credited with the maintenance of high morale throughout the existence of the camp.

Welfare

Representatives of the International Red Cross Committee and the Protecting Power visited the camp approximately every three months, and always transmitted the complaints of the MOC to the German authorities in a strong manner. On many occasions, the Representatives reported unsatisfactory conditions at the camp to the State Department, and made every attempt to correct such conditions at the time of the visits.

The dispatch of Red Cross parcels to the camps was prompt, and all delays in supplies reaching PW was blamed on the German authorities. On several occasions insufficient clothing supplies were dispatched, but this was usually due to an increase in the strength after the requisition had been received in Geneva.

Requisitions to the YMCA for sports equipment and books were always promptly filled. The only delay incurred on the requests was in getting the approval of transmission from the German commandant.

Religion

Even though repeated requests for additional chaplains were made to the German authorities, Captain Stephen W. Kane carried the full eclesiastical [sic] burden for the camp. The PW cooperated with Father Kane in converting a barrack into a chapel for the religious services. Father Kane held daily services for the Catholics of the camp, and offered additional services for the Protestant PW. His untiring efforts in behalf of the men contributed a great deal to the good morale and discipline of the camp.

Recreation

The large recreation area in the camp to which the men had access during most of the daylight hours permitted them to enjoy a number of sports. Basketball, volley ball, baseball, boxing and track meets were among the favorite outdoor exercises. In addition, some enterprising PW built a miniature golf course and used hockey sticks and handballs as equipment. Competitive spirit was high after barrack leagues and teams were formed. In addition to these activities, the PW took great pride in the excellent band which gave frequent concerts and which played for the theatrical efforts of the "Cardboard Players." During the colder months, the PW depended a great deal on card games, checkers, chess, and other indoor games, as well as reading material from the well-stocked library. A complete public address system with speakers in each barrack inspired the organization of a "radio station" (WPBS) which furnished scheduled programs of music and information.

The most outstanding effort in field of recreation was the educational program organized by T/Sgt. Alexander M. Haddon with the following aims and objectives:

(1) To keep men mentally alert
(2) To offer accredited instruction
(3) To help men to plan for post-war educational and vocational activities.

Sgt. Haddon was assisted by a staff composed of instructors, librarians, a secretary, and office help. Classes in Mathematics, Law, Photography, Music, Economics, American History, Shorthand, Auto Mechanics, English, Spanish, German and French were given to the students. The school was held in a building containing the fiction and technical libraries. Six separate classrooms accommodating 40 men were used for instruction, and furniture consisted of benches, tables and blackboards. Because the limited supply of technical books prevented a check-out system, tables and benches were furnished for reference work.

Interests which were not handled in the scheduled classes named above were provided for in evening discussion groups. These were usually journalism, farm management and live-stock farming, and were directed by men who had had successful experience in the fields. These evening discussion groups were particularly popular during the spring and summer months when they could be held outdoors after the supper hour.

When the school was first started, attendance registered 1389, but gradually enthusiasm dropped until the average attendance was 980. This was the average attendance figure during the school's operation.

Evacuation

On 8 April 1945, 4000 of the PW at Stalag 17B began an 18-day march of 281 miles to Braunau, Austria. The remaining 200 men were too ill to make the march and were left behind in the hospital. These men were liberated on 9 May 1945 by the Russians.

The marching column was divided into eight groups of 500 with an American leader in charge of each group guarded by about 20 German Volkssturm guards and two dogs. Red Cross parcels were issued to each man in sufficient amounts to last about seven days. During the 18-day march, the column averaged 20 kilometers each day. At the end of the day, they were forced to bivouac in open fields regardless of the weather. On three occasions, the men were quartered in cow barns. The only food furnished to PW by the German authorities was barley soup and bread. Trading with the German and Austrian civilians became the main source of sustenance after the Red Cross parcel supplies were exhausted. The destination of the column was a Russian prison camp 4 kilometers north of Braunau. Upon arrival the PW cut down pine trees and made small huts since there was no housing available. Roaming guards patrolled the area and the woods surrounding the area, but no escape attempts were made because it was apparent that the liberation forces were in the immediate vicinity.

The day after their arrival at the new site, Red Cross parcels were issued to every PW. A second issue was made a few days later of one parcel for every fifth man.

Liberation

On 3 May 1945 the camp was liberated when six men of the 13th Armored Division arrived in three jeeps and easily captured the remaining guards who numbered 205. Other units of the 13th Armored followed shortly and organized the evacuation of the PW by C-47 to France on 9 May 1945.

AMERICAN PRISONERS OF WAR IN GERMANY

Prepared by Military Intelligence Service War Department 15 July 1944 [Stalag Luft 4 and Stalag Luft 6 were not included in the War Department's postwar report of 1 November 1945.]

STALAG LUFT 4

Strength
1,482 AAF NCO's.

Location
Pin-point: 53° 55' North latitude.
                    16° 15' East longitude.
The camp is at Gross Tychow, Pomerania, 20 kilometers Southeast of Belgard.

Description
Opened to Americans on 12 May 1944, this new camp is only one quarter completed. Its eventual capacity will be 6,400. Ps/W are living in new wooden barracks where ventilation is at present insufficient but will soon be improved, according to the German commandant. Bathing facilities are not yet finished and Ps/W are unable to bathe. Toilet facilities are adequate. The Swiss delegate thinks the camp will be satisfactory when completed.

Treatment   Unknown.

Food
Ps/W complain about the food situation. They do not handle the administration of Red Cross parcels and have asked the Swiss delegate to protest against the present system to the German High Command. In addition, the camp lacks facilities for individual preparation of Red Cross food.

Clothing
The clothing supply is insufficient, pending the arrival of Red Cross shipments.

Health
Two American doctors are in charge of the temporary camp infirmary. Need of a dental office has been foreseen but none has yet been installed.

Religion
A chaplain has been requested.

Personnel   Unknown.

Mail

Mail arrives irregularly.

Recreation

A sports field lies within the camp, but there is no organized recreation, no theater and no canteen. YMCA representatives recently visited the camp.

Work

NCO's are not required to work.

Pay   Not known.

STALAG LUFT 6

Strength

2,411 AAF NCO's.

Location

Pin-point: 55° 21' North latitude.
               15° 19' 30" East longitude.
The camp is near the old Prussian-Lithuanian border at Heydekrug, 48 kilometers Northwest of Tilsit.

Description

The camp has three compounds: One American, another British, and the third joint British-American. The Britons are all RAF NCO's. Compounds contain ten stone-brick barracks, each with a capacity of 552 men, and 12 wooden huts each housing 54 Ps/W. Men sleep in double-decker bunks, have new tables, stools, lockers. Heating is satisfactory, but ventilation is bad because shutters must be kept closed due to police-dog patrols. A large laundry, a barrack serving as chapel and theater with eight small rooms for study, and seven infirmary barracks are centrally situated. With a barracks capacity of 6,168 men the camp now holds 10,400 Ps/W. It is believed 4,000 of these are quartered in tents.

Treatment   Correct.

Food

German rations are poor. The potato allowance has been reduced from 400 to 300 grams, the quality of turnips has deteriorated, and fresh vegetables are unknown. These shortcomings are critical in light of reports that Red Cross food stocks on which Ps/W are dependent were exhausted 10 May and have not been replenished. Food parcels are pooled and two hot meals prepared daily in each compound's kitchen. Lack of facilities in the kitchen makes communal preparation unsatisfactory while crowding obviates the possibility of individual preparation of food.

Clothing

Furnished by Red Cross. Worn-out clothing is supplied by Germans to Ps/W employed in camp. Sewing machines and cobblers' tools are badly needed.

Health

Health, now fair, is threatened by congestion. While good medical care is provided by two British medical officers, at least two more doctors and one dentist are essential. The infirmary which should have a minimum of 150 beds has only 70. As a result, many of the sick are hospitalized in their regular barracks. Washing and toilet facilities are satisfactory.

Religion

Three British chaplains hold services in the barrack chapel. At the request of the Ps/W the Camp Commandant has applied to his superiors for a Roman Catholic chaplain.

Personnel

Man of Confidence: T/Sgt. Francis S. Paules
Secretary: T/Sgt. Jos. H. Harrison
Camp Commandant: Oberst Hoermann Von-
                       Hoerbach

Mail

Average transit time for surface mail from camp to U.S.A. is nine weeks; airmail one month. Letters to camp from USA require two months travel time. Book parcels have been held at camp before distribution for periods up to six months because of too few censors.

Recreation

Although space for athletics is limited, Ps/W play baseball, football and other games for which YMCA has provided equipment. Educational courses are available with Ps/W instructors in subjects ranging from banking through foreign languages. Entertainment is provided by a band, a choir, and a dramatic group which presents occasional shows at the camp theater. The library has 6,000 books.

Work

Work is not required. Some Ps/W work of their own volition in the carpenter shop, making clothespins for the central laundry.

Pay   Not known.

SELECT BIBLIOGRAPHY

PRIMARY SOURCES

Manuscripts

Army Air Force P.O.W. Exposition Scrapbook, n.d. U.S. Military History Institute, Carlisle, PA.

Greening, C. Ross and Angelo M. Spinelli. *The Yankee Kriegies*, n.d. National Council of Young Men's Christian Associations, New York, NY.

I Was in Prison, n.d. World's Alliance of Young Men's Christian Association, Geneva, Switzerland.

Military Intelligence Service. *Report on American Prisoners of War in Germany*, 15 July 1944. American Red Cross Headquarters Archives, Washington, DC.

_____. *Report on American Prisoners of War in Germany*, 1 November 1945. American Red Cross Headquarters Archives, Washington, DC.

Robinson, Arthur. *The History of the American National Red Cross, Volume XXII: Relief to Prisoners of War in World War II*, 1950. American Red Cross Headquarters Archives, Washington, DC.

Weaver, Blanche Henry Clark. *The History of the American National Red Cross and Other Agencies in Sending Relief to Prisoners of War*, 1950. American Red Cross Headquarters Archives, Washington, DC.

Books

Bailey, Ronald H. *Prisoners of War*. Alexandria, VA: Time-Life Books, 1981.

Bowman, Martin W. *Home By Christmas?* Wellingborough, Northamptonshire, England: Patrick Stephens, 1987.

Boyle, J.B. *Excerpts From A Kriegie Log*. Cazenovia, NY: J.B. Boyle, 1965.

Diggs, J. Frank. *The Welcome Swede*. New York: Vantage Press, 1988.

Durand, Arthur A. *Stalag Luft III*. Baton Rouge, LA: Louisiana State University Press, 1988.

Greening, Charles Ross. *Not As Briefed*. St. Paul, MN: Brown & Bigelow, n.d.

Huff, Russell J. *Wings of World War II*. Sarasota, FL: R.J. Huff & Assoc., Inc., 1985.

Kimball, R.W., and O.M. Chiesl. *Clipped Wings*. Dayton, OH: R. W. Kimball, 1948.

Roy, Morris J. *Behind Barbed Wire*. New York: Richard R. Smith, 1946.

Rumpf, Hans. *The Bombing of Germany*. Translated by Edward Fitzgerald. New York: Holt, Rinehart & Winston, 1962.

Simmons, Kenneth W. *Kriegie*. New York: Thomas Nelson & Sons, 1960.

Toliver, Raymond F. *The Interrogator*. Encino, CA: Raymond F. Toliver, 1978.

Welcome to POW Camp Stalag Luft I, Barth, Germany. Raleigh, NC: Edwards & Broughton Co., n.d.

Zemke, Hubert (as told to Roger A. Freeman). *Zemke's Stalag*. Washington, DC: Smithsonian Institution Press, 1991.

Interviews

Adams, John. Telephone interview with author. 20 September 1993.

Bogue, Hardy Z. III. Interview with author. Charlottesville, VA. 8 March 1994.

Boyle, Joseph.Telephone interview with author. 23 July 1994.

Burkhart, John. Telephone interview with author. 3 October 1993.

Cline, Claire. Telephone interview with author. 12 February 1994.

Fishburne, Dorothy. Telephone interview with author. 30 January 1994.

Friend, John. Interview with author. New York, NY. 17 September 1994.

Gorsky, Henry. Telephone interview with author. 5 February 1994.

Griffin, Thomas C. Interview with author. Cincinnati, OH. 11 September 1994.

Keller, Robert. Interview with author. Charlottesville, VA. 11 October 1994.

Kroos, Arthur. Telephone interview with author. 12 February 1994.

Lian, Elmer T. Telephone interview with author. 12 February 1994.

Mankie, James. Interview with author. Charlottesville, VA. 20 August 1993.

McVicker, Robert. Interview with author. Alexandria, VA. 23 July 1993.

Reams, Patrick. Telephone interview with author. 17 July 1994.

Ricci, Al. Telephone interview with author. 12 February 1994.

Stenger, Charles. Telephone interview with author. 3 February 1994.

Stewart, Richard. Interview with author. Spotsylvania, VA. 6 July 1994.

Wendell, Roy E. Interview with author. Melville, NY. 6 August 1993.

Wilkerson, Daniel. Telephone interview with author. 26 January 1994.

Williams, Charles. Interview with author. Washington, DC. 1 September 1993.

Wodicka, Edward. Interview with author. Stanardsville, VA. 21 October 1993.

Wartime Log Books

Adams, John. *A Wartime Log.* Personal Collection.

Belk, Claudius. *A Wartime Log.* Collection of Norm Flayderman.

Cohen, Sylvan. *A Wartime Log.* Collection of Hardy Z. Bogue III.

Friend, John. *A Wartime Log.* Personal Collection.

Greening, C. Ross. *A Wartime Log.* Collection of Dorothy Fishburne.

Griffin, Thomas C. *A Wartime Log.* Personal Collection.

Martin, Joseph W. E. *A Wartime Log.* Collection of Art Beltrone.

McVicker, Robert A. *A Wartime Log.* Personal Collection.

Reams, Patrick. *A Wartime Log.* Collection of U.S. Army Military History Institute, Carlisle, PA.

Stewart, Richard. *A Wartime Log.* Personal Collection.

Wendell, Roy E. *A Wartime Log.* Personal Collection.

Wilkerson, Daniel. *A Wartime Log* (British edition). Personal Collection.

Williams, Charles. *A Wartime Log.* Personal Collection.

Wodicka, Edward. *A Wartime Log.* Personal Collection.

Other Logs

Franklyn, Howard N. Soft-covered booklet. Collection of Art Beltrone.

Keller, Robert. Soft-covered booklet. Personal Collection.

Kroos, Arthur. Soft-covered booklet. Personal Collection.

Lian, Elmer T. Soft-covered booklet. Personal Collection.

Mankie, James. Soft-covered booklet. Personal Collection.

Other Sources

Ricci, Al. *Ritbok.* Personal Collection.

Correspondence

Danthe, Claude-Alain. Letter to author. 3 August 1993.

Soderberg, Henry. Letters to author. 5 November 1993 and 5 December 1993.

INDEX

A

Adams, John Howard, 34, 63
Aircrew positions: bombardier, 26;
    copilot, 28; gunner, 27, 28;
    pilot, 28; radio operator, 27
Air Force Museum (United
    States), 170
"Air Gangsters," 31, 42
American Prisoners of War in
    Germany, reports, 70, 174-
    203
Anderson, Andrew, 13
Appel, 81, 107, 148
Arts and crafts, 109, 110, 112,
    135, 146, 171
Associations, American prisoner of
    war, 11
Athletic equipment, 122, 125, 150
Augsburg, 30
Avignon, 43

B

B-17, 15, 22, 23, 27, 29, 30, 31,
    37, 38, 39, 43
B-24, 24, 37
B-26, 32, 108
Bamberg, 45
Baron, the, 38, 45, 46
Barracks, 52-53, 54, 58-59, 70,
    90, 107, 108, 111, 114, 119,
    122, 126, 148
Barth, 68, 112
Barth Hard Times, 165
Bartlett, Lt. J. A., 8
Belk, Claudius, 20, 54, 57, 61, 63,
    84, 87, 142
Berlin, 46
"Birdmen," 34, 70
Books, library, 6, 36, 133
Boredom, 2, 58-59
Boyle, Joseph, 79, 90, 117-118,
    126, 149-151
Braunau, 162
Breidenthal, Les, 133

Burkhart, John R., 108-109

C

Cards, playing, 2, 80, 93
Cars, designing, 135
Cartooning, 117
Cartoons, 31, 37, 42, 44, 60, 61,
    62, 63, 68, 78-79, 84, 86, 87,
    89, 91, 93, 94, 95, 102, 115,
    119, 125, 127, 130, 131, 142,
    147, 151, 159, 163
Cecil, Lt. R. C., 8
Cell, solitary confinement, 65, 66,
    171
Chess, 92
Christmas, 77, 144
Churchill, Winston, 77
Cigarettes, 28, 39, 96, 126
Circuit, the, 117
Cline, Claire, 156, 168
Clothing, 63, 67, 87, 117, 132
Coal rations, 84
Cohen, Sylvan, 15, 19, 23, 25, 27,
    28, 29, 39, 48, 51, 54, 80,
    100, 111, 116, 143, 146, 161
Cologne, 46
Combat, aerial, 23, 24, 25, 26, 29,
    31, 32, 35, 38, 42, 43
Comedians, 129, 131
Cooler, the, 57, 64, 150

D

D-bar, chocolate, 39, 102-103,
    104, 117, 126, 153
Deaths, prisoner, 90, 173
Dedmon, Emmett, 159
Dogfight, 35
Dogs, guard, 148
Dog tags, 88, 115
Donald Duck, prisoner symbol,
    31, 60-61, 84
Dorfman, Lt. J. A., 8
Dottie G, 30
Dresden, 151

Dubendorf Air Field, 30
Dulag Luft, 57, 66, 69

E

Einstein, Albert, 168
Entertainment, 124, 125, 129,
    131, 132, 156
Equipment, athletic, 36, 119, 122,
    125, 150, 151
Escape materials, 132, 133
Esquire, 27, 28, 39

F

Ferrets, 148, 149
Fishburne, Dorothy, 110
Flak, 29, 38, 43
Flowers, 20
Focke-Wulf FW 190, 25, 29, 38
Food: packaging plants, 98;
    recipes, 102-103; restaurants,
    83, 120; quantity and quality,
    13, 97-99, 101, 102, 115,
    122, 124, 126, 148, 151, 162,
    166; transportation, 100-102
Frankfurt, 45, 46, 65, 66
Freight cars, 50-51, 100, 101, 102,
    162
Friend, John, 24, 31, 49, 57, 65,
    87, 90, 131, 132, 144, 162
Funerals, camp, 173

G

Geneva, 75, 99, 100, 101
Geneva Convention, provisions
    of, 70-74, 97
Gestapo, 149
Glenn, Carol, 168
Golf, 150-151
Goodrich, Col., 164
Goon-baiting, 146, 148, 149, 150,
    151
Greening, Lt. Col. Charles Ross,
    24, 32, 51, 53, 81, 82, 88, 92,
    93, 95, 108-110, 112, 135, 141

Griffin, Thomas, 162-164, 166

H

Holmstrom, Lt. C. H., 6
Humor, 31, 37, 42, 62, 63, 68,
    78-79, 89, 91, 92, 93, 94, 95,
    102, 115, 121, 127, 129, 132,
    142, 146-151, 159

I

Ice Skating, 119, 149
Ingenuity, prisoner, 102-103, 108-
    110, 132, 150-151, 152-155,
    156, 158-159, 165, 168, 170,
    171
Insignia, See Wings
Internees, 30
Interrogation, 31, 66, 68

K

Keller, Robert, 132, 133, 140
Kious, Lt. H. E., 8
Kriegie, 79, 110, 127
Kriegie Kraft Karnival, 109, 110,
    135
Kriegsbrot, 53
Kriegsgefangenen, 110

L

LaGuardia, Fiorello H., 168
Landscapes, 20, 112, 143
Latrine, 84, 119, 151
Letters, 108, 111, 120, 121, 140,
    141
Lian, Elmer T., 152-153
Liberation, 160, 162-166
Libraries, camp, 150
Life With Father, 4
Liquor, 117
List, Eugene, 168
Loneliness, 141, 144
Long, Robert A., 30

M

Maher, Lt. D. J., 8
Mankie, James, 17, 102
Mannheim, 152
Martin, Earl, 97
Martin, Joseph W.E., 30
McVicker, Robert, 2, 35, 46, 119,
    122, 151
Medals, sports, 150
Messerschmitt Bf 109, 38, 110
Messerschmitt Bf 110, 30
Mess hall, 82, 109, 117
Military Intelligence Service, War
    Department, 70, 174
Military tradition: American, 148;
    German, 146, 148
Moosburg, 13, 102, 162, 166
Mount Vesuvius, 32, 108
Munich, 101, 102
Museum of Science and Industry,
    168, 170
Musical instruments, 124, 156,
    168
Muskau, 162, 164

N

"No man's land," 54
Not As Briefed, 110
Notre Dame, 151

O

Oberursel, 66
O.K., 114

P

P-51, 110
Phelper, Ben, 39
Poetry, 33, 58, 63, 65, 77, 97,
    101, 118, 140, 145, 158-159,
    172; writing, 118
"P.O.W. Exposition," Army Air
    Force, 168; exhibition loca-
    tions and dates, 170
Price, Lt. Linden, 8

Prisoners of War Bulletin, 71
Prisoners of war: camp life, 71;
    numbers of, 70
Propaganda, 43, 167

Q

Queen Mary, 68

R

Reams, Patrick, 17, 19, 103, 121,
    126, 148, 159, 163
Red Cross: 14, 19, 66, 97-103,
    121; capture parcel, 67; food
    parcel, 97, 98, 99, 102, 103,
    117, 122, 151, 164;
    International Committee, 74,
    100; International
    Committee, Relief Division,
    101; *Prisoners of War Bulletin*,
    71; ships, 98, 100; volunteers,
    98
Regan, James R., 140
Religion, 19, 150
Republic Aviation Corporation,
    135
Restaurants, 83, 120
Ricci, Al, 110, 112-113
Roll call, 81, 107, 146, 148
Rumors, 119, 142, 162
Russians, 151, 162, 165

S

"Sack," the, 63, 78-79, 95
St. Elizabeth's Lazarette, 46
Shaft, the, 117
Singing, 124, 132
Softball, 122, 124
Solingen, 28
Solitary confinement, 65, 66, 150
Spinazzola, 37
Sports, 36, 72, 122, 124, 125, 150
Spremberg, 162
Stalag 7A, 13, 160, 162, 164
Stalag 13D, 162

Stalag 17B, 27, 28, 51, 54, 115, 146, 161, 162

Stalag Luft I, 4, 13, 17, 24, 32, 34, 42, 53, 57, 59, 65, 68, 70, 81, 82, 83, 95, 108, 109, 110, 112, 113, 126, 129, 135, 138, 139, 144, 146, 148, 150, 151, 154, 155, 156, 162, 165

Stalag Luft III, 6, 8, 13, 57, 61, 63, 73, 84, 87, 90, 97, 104, 126, 133, 140, 149, 150, 162, 163, 173

Stalag Luft 4, 46, 115, 119, 159

Standard Food Package, 97-103, 122, 151, 166

Stenger, Charles A., 70, 78, 146

Stewart, Richard A., 19, 20, 38, 45, 46, 68, 96, 114, 115, 119, 121, 135, 136, 137

Stooge, 104

Stoves, prisoner-made, 13, 135, 152

Stuttgart, 110

Sweetie Girl, 37, 38

T

Theater: 4, 124, 125, 131-133, 150; productions, 125, 131-132; programs, 4; supplies, 124

Thunderbolt, 135

Tower, guard, 49, 55, 90, 113, 128

Trading, 39, 96, 104, 126, 127, 136

Trenches, air raid, 51

Tunnels, escape, 122, 146

V

Vegetables, 113

Vienna, 37

Violin, prisoner-made, 156, 168

W

Walt Disney Studios, 61

War Prisoners Aid News, 77

War Prisoners Aid, Y.M.C.A., 14, 36, 77, 108, 122, 125, 149

Wartime Log: American, 36, 46, 77, 78, 84, 97, 101, 103, 104, 107, 108, 110, 112, 114, 117, 119, 120, 121, 126, 150, 162, 168; British, 17, 36, 124; Canadian, 36; cover letter, 16; soft-covered, 17, 36;

Washing, clothes, 86, 87

Wasmer, Henry, 101

Wendell, Roy E. Jr., 19, 65, 66, 68, 78, 95, 107, 146, 151

Wetzlar, 66

Wiench, Lt. A. H., 8

Wilkerson, Daniel D. Jr., 103, 122, 124

Williams, Charles, 37-38

Wings: examples of, 136-139, 153-155; manufacture of, 152-153

Wodicka, Edward S., 15, 20, 31, 37, 43, 44, 61, 63, 84, 89, 95, 97, 104, 107, 116

Women: drawings of, 94, 95, 116, 121, 130, 140, 141

Y

Y.M.C.A.: 14, 17, 19, 36, 78, 119, 122, 124, 150; medal, 110, 112, 150; publication, 153; supplies, 36, 125

Yankee Kriegies, 153

Z

Zavisho, John E., 133